REVELATION
FROM START2FINISH

MICHAEL WHITWORTH

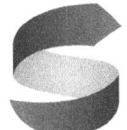

© 2025 by Start2Finish

All rights reserved. No part of this publication may be reproduced, stored in a retrieval system, or transmitted in any form or by any means without the prior written permission of the author. The only exception is brief quotations in printed reviews.

ISBN 978-1-941972-87-8

Published by Start2Finish
Bend, Oregon 97702
start2finish.org

Printed in the United States of America

Unless otherwise noted, all Scripture quotations are from The Holy Bible, English Standard Version®, copyright © 2001 by Crossway Bibles, a publishing ministry of Good News Publishers. Used by permission. All rights reserved.

Cover Design: Evangela Creative

CONTENTS

1.	Introduction to Revelation	5
2.	The Vision of the Risen Christ	13
3.	Letters to the Churches, Pt. 1	21
4.	Letters to the Churches, Pt. 2	29
5.	The Throne & the Lamb	37
6.	The Seals & the Redeemed	45
7.	Trumpets of Judgment	53
8.	The Little Scroll & Two Witnesses	61
9.	The Dragon & the Beasts	69
10.	The Harvest & the Bowls	77
11.	The Fall of Babylon	87
12.	The Marriage & the Millennium	95
13.	The New Heaven & New Earth	103

1

INTRODUCTION TO REVELATION

Objective: To equip believers to understand Revelation's background, message, and enduring call to worship and faithfulness.

INTRODUCTION

When the Roman Empire reached the height of its power, it seemed indestructible. Its armies marched unchallenged, its cities flourished, and its emperors claimed divine honor. Yet on a rocky island in the Aegean Sea, an old man exiled for his faith began to write. His world appeared dominated by Caesar's might, but his vision opened into heaven itself. What he saw changed how the church would see history forever.

Few books of Scripture have generated more fascination—and more confusion—than the book of Revelation. Its images of dragons, beasts, trumpets, and thrones have both inspired and intimidated generations of believers. Some have approached it with curiosity, trying to decode the future; others, with fear, as though it were a map of impending doom. But Revelation is neither a puzzle to solve nor a horror story to dread. It is a letter written to ordinary Christians facing extraordinary pressure—a word of hope, warning, and worship.

Revelation is not about escape from the world but perseverance within it. It reminds the church that God still reigns when empires roar, that

Christ still wins when evil appears strong, and that the people of God can endure because their future is secure. Its ultimate message is simple and stunning: the Lamb reigns, the faithful endure, and evil will not last.

EXAMINATION

Authorship and audience (1:1-3)

Revelation begins, "The revelation of Jesus Christ, which God gave him to show to his servants the things that must soon take place." From the opening line, the book presents itself not as a mystery to hide but as a message to reveal. The term "revelation" (Greek *apokalypsis*) means "unveiling"—pulling back the curtain to show reality from heaven's perspective.

The author identifies himself as "John." Early Christian tradition overwhelmingly affirms that this John is the apostle, the beloved disciple of Jesus and author of the Fourth Gospel and the three Epistles of John. Christian writers such as Justin Martyr, Irenaeus, and Tertullian—figures from the second century who lived close to Revelation's original setting—affirmed Johannine authorship. The vivid imagery, deep knowledge of the Old Testament, and pastoral concern for local congregations all fit what we know of the apostle's heart and style.

Revelation was written "to the seven churches that are in Asia" (1:4). These were real congregations in western Asia Minor (modern Turkey): Ephesus, Smyrna, Pergamum, Thyatira, Sardis, Philadelphia, and Laodicea. The number seven represents completeness, suggesting that the message extends beyond these churches to the entire body of Christ. The believers in Asia faced a culture steeped in idolatry, prosperity, and political loyalty to Rome. The imperial cult—worshiping the emperor as divine—had become a civic expectation. Refusing to participate could cost one's trade, freedom, or life.

John wrote to encourage perseverance and faithfulness in a society that demanded compromise. Each church received a specific message reflecting its condition—some faithful, some lukewarm, some deceived by false teaching. Through them all, Christ walked "among the lampstands," fully present with his people. Revelation is therefore both local and universal, historical and timeless.

Date and setting

Most scholars place Revelation near the end of the first century, around AD 95, during the reign of Emperor Domitian. Domitian was not the first emperor to claim divinity, but he demanded it more systematically than any before him. Citizens were expected to address him as "Lord and God." In such an environment, confessing "Jesus is Lord" was not merely religious language—it was an act of resistance and rebellion.

John was exiled to the island of Patmos, a rocky outcrop in the Aegean Sea used by Rome as a penal colony. There, cut off from his congregations, he received the visions that form this book. Revelation was written from exile to the persecuted, from isolation to the scattered, from a prison to a church under pressure. It was meant to be read aloud in public worship and to be understood by the very people for whom it was written.

Some scholars argue for an earlier date under Nero's persecution (AD 64–68), but internal clues favor the later setting. The churches show signs of maturity and second-generation leadership; persecution has become organized; and the imperial power behind Babylon clearly mirrors Rome at its height. Regardless of the precise date, the context remains the same: believers needed assurance that God was still in control when the world seemed ruled by cruelty.

The nature of apocalyptic literature

Revelation belongs to a literary genre known as *apocalyptic*, common among Jewish writings between 200 BC and AD 100. The word *apokalypsis* means "unveiling." Apocalyptic writings reveal heavenly realities behind earthly events. They use symbols, visions, and cosmic imagery to express truth about God's rule and humanity's destiny.

Apocalyptic literature arises during times of crisis, when God's people face oppression and need reassurance that evil will not have the final word. Books like Daniel, Ezekiel, and Zechariah use similar language—beasts, thrones, angels, and numbers. These are not meant to conceal meaning but to express it in imagery beyond literal description.

Revelation, then, is not a codebook of future headlines but a picture book of spiritual truths. Its symbols are the language of the oppressed: metaphors that speak of hope when direct speech could be dangerous. The beasts represent empires; Babylon represents the seductive power of worldly culture; the number seven represents perfection; the number twelve, the people of God.

Understanding Revelation as apocalyptic helps readers avoid two extremes—taking every image literally or dismissing them as mere fantasy. Symbols communicate reality through imagination. When John saw the Lamb on the throne, he was not watching an animal but perceiving the victorious Christ. Apocalyptic literature calls believers to see the unseen—to view history through heaven's eyes.

The four major interpretive approaches

For nearly two thousand years, Christians have interpreted Revelation through four main lenses. Each approach highlights an aspect of truth but risks distortion if taken exclusively.

1. The Preterist View. Preterists understand most of Revelation as describing events that occurred in the first century. The book was written to encourage persecuted Christians under Rome and to announce God's coming judgment on their oppressors. Babylon symbolizes Rome; the beast, imperial power; the false prophet, imperial religion. The preterist view emphasizes that Revelation meant something concrete to its original audience and that "the things that must soon take place" (1:1) did indeed happen soon for them. Its strength lies in historical grounding—it keeps the message anchored in its first-century context. However, it can risk reducing Revelation to ancient history, leaving little room for its continuing relevance.

2. The Historicist View. This approach interprets Revelation as a prophetic outline of church history from the first century to the end of time. Each vision corresponds to a specific era—the fall of Rome, the rise of Islam, the Reformation, modern missions, and so forth. This view once dominated Protestant thought, especially among reformers who identified the papacy with the beast. Its strength is its conviction that Revelation speaks across history, but its weakness is speculation. Attempts to align every symbol with a specific century often reflect the interpreter's era more than John's intent.

3. The Futurist View. The futurist sees most of Revelation (chapters 4–22) as describing events still to come—the Great Tribulation, the rise of the Antichrist, and Christ's millennial reign. This approach dominates popular Christian imagination today, thanks to centuries of premillennial teaching and modern media portrayals. It reminds readers that God's purposes will culminate in a real, future return of Christ. Yet it can unintentionally shift the focus away from Revelation's pastoral message to its original readers. If the book only applies to future generations, the seven churches might as well have been irrelevant.

4. The Idealist (or Symbolic) View. The idealist sees Revelation as a timeless drama of the conflict between good and evil, the kingdom of God and the powers of darkness. Its images symbolize recurring realities—the arrogance of empire, the perseverance of the saints, the deceit of idolatry, and the final victory of Christ. This view emphasizes spiritual truth rather than historical prediction. Its weakness lies in vagueness; its strength, in universality.

A balanced approach combines the best insights of all four. Revelation spoke first to real churches in the first century (preterist), has spoken to the church throughout history (historicist), will find ultimate fulfillment in Christ's return (futurist), and continues to unveil spiritual realities in every generation (idealist). Above all, Revelation is about Jesus Christ, not about beasts, timelines, or disasters. The opening line names its subject clearly: "The revelation of Jesus Christ."

The theological themes of Revelation

Revelation's theology is not new; it is the climax of Scripture's story. From Genesis to Revelation, God reveals himself as Creator, Redeemer, and King. Several themes run through every vision.

The Sovereignty of God. From start to finish, the throne dominates Revelation's landscape. Empires rise and fall, but the throne never trembles. Even the forces of evil operate under divine permission. The Lamb opens the seals; the angels sound the trumpets; the bowls of wrath come from heaven's temple. Nothing happens apart from God's will. For a suffering church, that truth was their anchor: the universe is not governed by chaos, but by Christ.

The Victory of the Lamb. John expected to see a lion and instead saw a lamb (5:6). That moment defines the book. The power of God is revealed through sacrifice, not domination. The Lamb conquers by being slain.

Revelation presents history's greatest paradox: victory through vulnerability. The faithful follow the same path—they conquer "by the blood of the Lamb and by the word of their testimony" (12:11).

The Call to Endurance. Revelation is a manual for perseverance. Its refrain appears throughout: "To the one who conquers…" Each letter to the churches ends with that call. Endurance is not passive waiting but active faithfulness—resisting compromise, enduring hardship, and holding fast to hope. The crown of life belongs to those who endure.

Worship as Resistance. Every scene in heaven contrasts with scenes on earth. While the world worships the beast, heaven worships the Lamb. Worship is therefore not escape but defiance—it declares that Caesar is not Lord. The church's songs become its strongest weapon. In Revelation, worship dethrones idols by giving God his rightful glory.

Judgment and Renewal. God's judgment is not vindictive but redemptive. It purges evil to make room for renewal. The plagues, trumpets, and bowls lead to the final vision of new creation, where "the dwelling place of God is with man." The story ends not in despair but in restoration—the garden restored, the curse undone, and the Lamb enthroned.

APPLICATION

1. Revelation trains the church to see clearly

In every age, believers must discern the difference between the Lamb's kingdom and Babylon's empire. Revelation sharpens that vision. It teaches the church to recognize idolatry disguised as patriotism, greed disguised as prosperity, and compromise disguised as peace. By seeing the world through heaven's eyes, Christians learn to live with courage and clarity in a culture that still worships power.

2. Revelation gives courage in the face of suffering

The first-century believers lived under the shadow of persecution; many in our time still do. Revelation assures them that suffering is never wasted. The Lamb who reigns also suffered. His scars are his crown, and so will be ours. The book calls Christians to endure, not because evil is strong, but because its time is short.

3. Revelation reorients worship and witness

At its heart, Revelation is a call to worship. Every time the church gathers at the Lord's table or sings the Lamb's praise, it proclaims to the powers of the world that Jesus is Lord. Worship fuels witness, and witness sustains worship. The church's task is not to predict headlines but to live as a prophetic community that embodies hope.

4. Revelation restores confidence in God's future

The last word of Scripture is not uncertainty but assurance. "Surely I am coming soon," says Jesus. The church answers, "Amen. Come, Lord Jesus." Hope is not wishful thinking but faithful expectation. Because the Lamb reigns, believers can live in the present with peace and purpose.

CONCLUSION

Revelation is not a book to be feared, but one to be cherished. It was written to comfort the afflicted, to warn the complacent, and to strengthen the faithful. Its message spans all time: God rules, the Lamb triumphs, the church must endure, and the new creation is certain.

From the garden to the city, from exile to homecoming, the story of Scripture ends where it began—with God dwelling among his people. The throne stands, the curse is gone, and the song of heaven fills eternity. Until that day, believers live as those who already know the ending. The Spirit and the Bride still say, "Come."

REFLECTION

1. What circumstances might have made Revelation's message urgent for the churches of Asia?

2. How does understanding apocalyptic language help you read Revelation faithfully?

3. Which interpretive approach best balances historical context and timeless truth?

4. What does the victory of the Lamb teach about power, leadership, and faithfulness?

5. Why is worship the church's most powerful response to fear and persecution?

6. How can Revelation's hope sustain your faith and endurance in today's world?

DISCUSSION

1. How does knowing Revelation was written to real first-century churches change how we read it today?

2. What features of apocalyptic literature make it both challenging and powerful for modern readers?

3. Which of the four interpretive approaches (preterist, historicist, futurist, idealist) most resonates with you, and why?

4. How does the image of the Lamb redefine our understanding of victory and strength?

5. What does it mean for worship to act as resistance against the powers of our culture?

6. In what ways can the church live as a preview of God's new creation here and now?

2

THE VISION OF THE RISEN CHRIST

REVELATION 1

Objective: To encourage Christians to live fearlessly and faithfully, trusting the risen Christ's presence and authority.

INTRODUCTION

In the early days of the Apollo space program, astronaut James Irwin stood on the surface of the moon and gazed back at Earth—a glowing blue sphere suspended in blackness. When he returned home, Irwin said that the experience forever changed his perspective on life's problems: "When you've walked on the moon and looked back at Earth, everything else seems small."

That sense of awe and perspective captures what happens in Revelation 1. John, exiled on the island of Patmos, received a vision that lifted his eyes from the hardship of persecution to the majesty of heaven's throne. The curtain between the earthly and the eternal was pulled back, and John beheld the risen Christ in all his glory.

The vision was overwhelming—blazing eyes, a roaring voice, and radiant splendor. Yet the message was deeply personal: "Fear not." The exalted Lord walks among his churches. He sees their suffering, sustains their faith, and reminds them that courage is possible because he reigns. Revelation begins not with confusion, but with comfort—a call to renewed faithfulness and fearless devotion to the Lamb who lives forever.

EXAMINATION

The revelation of Jesus Christ (1:1-3)

The book opens not with confusion, but with clarity. "The revelation of Jesus Christ" (Rev. 1:1) declares that what follows is an unveiling, not a riddle. The Greek term *apokalypsis* means disclosure—something hidden now revealed. This message comes from Jesus, about Jesus, and ultimately for his servants, "to show…the things that must soon take place." Far from a puzzle meant to intimidate, Revelation is divine encouragement for believers living between Christ's first and second comings.

John identifies the chain of communication: from God to Jesus, to his angel, to John, to the church. The opening verses assure us that this book is rooted in the authority of heaven itself. The blessing in verse 3—"Blessed is the one who reads aloud the words of this prophecy, and blessed are those who hear, and who keep what is written in it"—promises that Revelation is practical. It was not written for curiosity, but for obedience.

Revelation's prophecies are meant to be read in worship, heard in faith, and kept in life. The emphasis on "soon" reminds Christians that God's redemptive plan is already unfolding. "Soon" does not mean immediate in the human sense, but certain in the divine one. The end has already begun in Christ's resurrection. The churches of Asia Minor—and every generation since—live in the tension between tribulation and triumph.

Grace and peace from the triune God (1:4-8)

John's greeting resembles Paul's letters but expands into a majestic doxology. He writes "to the seven churches that are in Asia," symbolic of the whole church in every place and time. He invokes "grace to you and peace" from the eternal God—"him who is and who was and who is to come"—language drawn from Exodus 3:14. God's self-existence assures believers that their Lord is not bound by time or circumstance.

The Holy Spirit appears as "the seven spirits who are before his throne." This does not imply multiple spirits but the fullness and perfection of the one Spirit's presence and power. John then exalts Jesus Christ in a threefold way: "the faithful witness," "the firstborn of the dead," and "the ruler of kings on earth." Each phrase affirms his victory. As "faithful witness," he revealed God's truth and suffered for it. As "firstborn of the dead," he triumphed over death. As "ruler of kings," he reigns now, not merely in the future.

John cannot mention Christ without doxology: "To him who loves us and has freed us from our sins by his blood and made us a kingdom, priests to his God and Father, to him be glory and dominion forever and ever." In a world ruled by emperors demanding worship, John reminds his readers that they already belong to a greater kingdom. Their citizenship is in heaven, their calling priestly, and their King sovereign.

Verse 7 declares the theme of the entire book: "Behold, he is coming with the clouds, and every eye will see him." The persecuted believers of Asia Minor could endure because they knew the story's end—Christ will return in glory, and those who pierced him will mourn. The Alpha and Omega (1:8) speaks, confirming that the God who began creation will also finish redemption. Revelation is the story of that completion.

John's exile and Christ's presence (1:9–11)

John introduces himself not as an apostle or prophet, but as a "brother and partner in the tribulation and the kingdom and the patient endurance that are in Jesus." His self-description captures the reality of the church's experience between Christ's comings: suffering, sovereignty, and steadfastness all coexist.

Exiled on the island of Patmos "on account of the word of God and the testimony of Jesus," John endured persecution under the emperor Domitian around AD 95. Yet his isolation became the setting for revelation. "I was in the Spirit on the Lord's day," he writes, signaling a prophetic trance during worship. Even on a barren island, the Lord's Day remained sacred. The Roman Empire could banish John from Ephesus, but it could not separate him from the presence of Christ.

A commanding voice "like a trumpet" instructed him to write to seven churches—Ephesus, Smyrna, Pergamum, Thyatira, Sardis, Philadelphia, and Laodicea. These were real congregations facing real trials: compromise, persecution, complacency. But through them, Christ would address every congregation in every age.

The Son of Man among the lampstands (1:12–16)

When John turned toward the voice, he saw "seven golden lampstands," representing the churches (1:20). In the middle stood "one like a son of man," language from Daniel 7:13–14 that identifies Jesus as the divine ruler entrusted with everlasting dominion. The details of his appearance are symbolic, not literal:

- His long robe and golden sash mark priestly and royal dignity.
- His hair, "white as white wool," evokes Daniel's Ancient of Days, revealing his eternal wisdom and purity.
- His eyes "like a flame of fire" see through hypocrisy and darkness.
- His feet "like burnished bronze" convey judgment that crushes evil.
- His voice "like the roar of many waters" suggests irresistible authority.
- In his right hand he holds "seven stars," symbols of the angels or messengers of the churches.
- From his mouth comes a "sharp two-edged sword," representing the power of his word.
- His face "like the sun shining in full strength" overwhelms all creation with divine glory.

This vision communicates one truth: the persecuted church is not abandoned. Christ walks among his lampstands. He holds their leaders securely. His authority, wisdom, and presence surround them. The church's strength does not rest in political influence or worldly safety, but in the sovereign Christ who reigns unseen.

Do not be afraid (1:17–20)

John's reaction was the same as Daniel's centuries earlier: "When I saw him, I fell at his feet as though dead." Confronted with divine glory, even an apostle collapses. But Jesus' response reveals the heart of Revelation: "Fear not." These words, spoken by the one whose eyes blaze like fire, transform terror into comfort.

"Fear not, I am the first and the last, and the living one. I died, and behold I am alive forevermore, and I have the keys of Death and Hades." The phrase "first and last" identifies him with God himself (Isa. 44:6). The one who died is alive forever; the one who descended to the grave now holds its keys. Death no longer controls the destiny of the faithful.

Jesus then commissions John to "write therefore the things that you have seen, those that are and those that are to take place after this." Revelation's structure unfolds from this command: Christ's present rule ("those that are") and the unfolding of his purposes ("those that are to take place"). The mystery of the stars and lampstands is explained: the stars are the angels of the seven churches, and the lampstands are the churches themselves.

The meaning is unmistakable—Christ knows his churches, holds their messengers, and walks among them. In every age, through every trial, he remains present and sovereign.

The call to fearless faithfulness

Revelation's opening chapter sets the tone for the entire book. The Christian life is not a waiting room for escape but a battlefield for endurance. John's readers faced the seductive pressure of emperor worship, economic marginalization, and even death. To them—and to us—Christ's message is steady: Fear not.

The glory that overwhelmed John is the same power that sustains believers today. The Son of Man still walks among his lampstands, still sees the deeds of his people, still calls them to faithfulness. His eyes are not blind to suffering, and his hands never release his church. Revelation begins with fear, but it ends with confidence—the living Christ reigns, and therefore his people can live without fear.

APPLICATION

1. Christ's glory strengthens our courage

When John turned and saw the glorified Son of Man, his strength failed him. Yet the same Lord who revealed such majesty reached down and touched him, saying, "Fear not." Awe and intimacy coexist in Christ's presence. His blazing eyes and thundering voice are not meant to terrify his followers but to remind them that ultimate power belongs to him. For Christians facing hostility, ridicule, or loss, this vision renews courage. The greater our view of Christ's glory, the smaller our fears appear. He rules over every king and empire; therefore, believers can stand firm and speak truth without trembling. A church that worships the exalted Christ need not fear the world's threats, because the one who commands the universe stands among his people and calls them his own.

2. Christ's presence sustains the church

John saw Christ "in the midst of the lampstands." That detail changes everything. The seven churches represent the entire body of Christ across time and space. Though weak and imperfect, they were not alone. The Son of Man walked among them, tending their light and holding their messengers in his right hand. His nearness was not sentimental but sovereign—he oversees, corrects, and protects his people. Even in seasons of decline, conflict, or persecution, believers can take heart: Christ has not left his church. Our confidence does not rest in attendance numbers, programs, or influence, but in his abiding presence. He still knows our deeds, strengthens our faith, and disciplines us for our good. The lampstands may flicker, but they will never go dark while he stands among them.

3. Christ's victory conquers our fear

The risen Lord declared, "I died, and behold I am alive forevermore, and I have the keys of Death and Hades." Every human fear ultimately flows from death—the fear of loss, of pain, of endings. Christ confronted death and stripped it of authority. The one who holds its keys decides who enters and who leaves. For persecuted believers, that truth transformed dread into courage. Death could threaten them, but it could not claim them. The same is true for us. When the world intimidates or when grief feels unbearable, remember who reigns. Christ's resurrection redefines reality. Fear no longer governs the Christian's heart because the grave no longer governs destiny. To live is Christ, and to die is gain. His empty tomb still silences our trembling and calls us to steadfast hope.

4. Christ's word calls for obedience

Revelation begins with a promise of blessing—not to those who analyze its symbols, but to those who "hear and keep" its message. The book is pastoral before it is prophetic. Its visions aim to shape conduct, not curiosity. In an age of compromise and distraction, Christians must recover the discipline of obedience. Christ speaks with authority sharper than any sword, and his word exposes what must change. Faithfulness means more than endurance; it means active loyalty. When the church listens and responds, she embodies her Lord's light before a watching world. Revelation's purpose is not to satisfy speculation about the future but to summon holiness in the present. Those who obey that call join John's blessing and prove that the glory of the risen Christ still transforms hearts today.

CONCLUSION

Revelation begins where every disciple must begin—with a clear vision of Jesus Christ. Before John writes to the churches or describes the future, he reminds believers who holds the future. The risen Lord stands among his lampstands, guiding, correcting, and sustaining his people. His glory humbles us; his touch strengthens us. When trials test our courage or faith grows weary, we remember the hand that lifted John from the ground and still whispers, "Fear not." The church's hope does not rest in escaping hardship but in enduring it with confidence that Christ reigns. Faithfulness becomes possible when we see him as he truly is—the living one, victorious forever.

REFLECTION

1. What does Revelation 1 teach about the true source of courage in the Christian life?

2. How does John's description of Christ's glory reshape your understanding of who Jesus is today?

3. Why is it important that Christ walks "among the lampstands"?

4. In what ways does Christ's victory over death change how you view suffering and loss?

5. What blessing does Revelation 1:3 promise, and how can you experience it personally?

6. How can you cultivate a heart that both fears and trusts Christ at the same time?

DISCUSSION

1. What do you find most striking about the vision of the Son of Man in Revelation 1?

2. How can a congregation today reflect confidence that Christ is still present among his people?

3. What forms of persecution or pressure might cause believers to compromise their faithfulness?

4. Why is obedience emphasized so strongly at the beginning of Revelation?

5. How can this opening chapter prepare us to understand the rest of the book?

6. What practical habits can help believers replace fear with faithful endurance in daily life?

3

LETTERS TO THE CHURCHES, PT. 1

REVELATION 2

Objective: To call believers to renewed love, endurance, purity, and discernment as marks of fearless faithfulness.

INTRODUCTION

During the construction of the Golden Gate Bridge, engineers installed safety nets beneath the spans. Before the nets were in place, progress was slow—workers hesitated, aware that a single misstep could mean death. But once the nets were stretched below, work accelerated, and confidence returned. The difference wasn't in the men's skill but in their assurance of safety.

That image captures the purpose of Christ's words to the churches in Revelation 2. These believers lived and served in a world of constant danger—political pressure, false teaching, moral temptation. Yet the risen Lord wanted them to know that his presence surrounded them like those safety nets beneath the bridge. He knew their works, their struggles, and their fears.

Through the letters to Ephesus, Smyrna, Pergamum, and Thyatira, Jesus calls his people to renewed faithfulness and fearlessness. His voice exposes cold hearts, comforts the suffering, confronts compromise, and corrects false tolerance. Behind every word is both warning and assurance: the Lord walks among his churches, and his hands still hold their future secure.

EXAMINATION

Christ's words to the churches

Revelation 1 revealed the risen Christ walking among his lampstands, sovereign over every congregation. Now in chapters 2–3 he speaks directly to those churches, showing that his glory is not abstract but practical. The exalted Son of Man addresses real communities wrestling with temptation, persecution, and fatigue. Each letter follows the same structure: a title drawn from Christ's vision, a word of praise, a word of rebuke, a call to repentance, and a promise to "the one who conquers." These are not seven isolated notes but a single pastoral message: the Lord knows his people. He inspects their hearts, sees their deeds, and desires their endurance.

The first four letters—to Ephesus, Smyrna, Pergamum, and Thyatira—reveal the full range of challenges facing the church. They warn against losing love, succumbing to fear, embracing compromise, or tolerating corruption. Above all, they call believers to renewed faithfulness in the face of pressure.

The church that lost its first love (2:1–7)

Ephesus was the crown jewel of Asia—wealthy, influential, and religiously proud. Its massive temple to Artemis drew pilgrims from across the empire. Yet within that pagan city stood a small community dedicated to the true God. The church at Ephesus had an enviable pedigree: Paul had labored there for years (Acts 19), Timothy had ministered there, and John himself may have shepherded it. These believers were not casual in their devotion. They had resisted false apostles and opposed the immoral teaching of the Nicolaitans. Their theology was sharp, their discipline firm, their reputation strong.

But Christ, who walks among the lampstands, saw beneath the surface. "You have abandoned the love you had at first." Their zeal for truth had outpaced their affection for God and one another. They could expose heresy but had lost tenderness. Doctrinal precision without devotion had drained their vitality. Christ calls them to remember their early warmth, repent of cold formalism, and return to the works born of love. Without repentance, their lampstand would be removed—an image of spiritual extinction. Yet hope remains: those who overcome will eat from "the tree of life," restored access to the life once forfeited in Eden.

Ephesus reminds every generation that orthodoxy and affection must remain united. A church can win arguments and lose its soul. True faith burns with both conviction and compassion.

The church that suffered faithfully (2:8–11)

Smyrna's believers faced a different danger—not apathy but affliction. The city was famed for beauty, culture, and loyalty to Rome. Temples to the emperor stood at its heart, and citizens proudly declared, "Caesar is Lord." Christians who refused that confession became outcasts. Many were stripped of jobs, homes, and even life. To them Christ reveals himself as "the first and the last, who died and came to life." The Lord who conquered death speaks directly to those staring it in the face.

"I know your tribulation and your poverty (but you are rich)." The world saw destitution; heaven saw treasure. The Lord never promised relief from suffering but presence within it. He warns that imprisonment will come, yet limits it: "ten days." Their trial would be intense but temporary. The command is simple and costly—"Be faithful unto death." The reward surpasses all loss: "I will give you the crown of life." In a city where athletes wore laurel wreaths and emperors displayed golden diadems, Christ offers a crown that never fades.

To the persecuted, he adds reassurance: "The one who conquers will not be hurt by the second death." Physical death cannot touch those sealed for eternal life. Smyrna teaches that suffering, though bitter, refines faith and reveals wealth the world cannot measure.

The church that compromised with the world (2:12–17)

Pergamum, some sixty miles north of Smyrna, was the political capital of the province. Its acropolis loomed over the plain, crowned by temples to Zeus, Dionysus, and Asclepius. Above them all rose the imperial altar to Caesar—"where Satan's throne is." To live as a Christian there required courage. Christ commends them: "You hold fast my name, and you did not deny my faith even in the days of Antipas my faithful witness." Tradition remembers Antipas as a martyr burned alive for refusing to worship the emperor.

Yet even heroic churches can fall prey to compromise. Some in Pergamum embraced teaching "like that of Balaam," who enticed Israel into idolatry and immorality (Num. 25). Others followed the Nicolaitans, perhaps claiming that participation in pagan feasts was harmless. Compromise always begins with justification—"We must live in the world"—but ends in spiritual dullness. Christ warns that his word, sharper than any sword, will wage war against those who refuse to repent.

Still, mercy triumphs for the faithful. He promises "hidden manna" and "a white stone with a new name." Manna recalls God's provision in the wilderness; the white stone may symbolize acquittal or admission to a feast. Together they depict acceptance and intimacy—the nourishment and welcome of the kingdom. Pergamum reminds us that the greatest threat to the church seldom comes from persecution but from seduction.

The church that tolerated false teaching (2:18–29)

Thyatira, the smallest of the seven cities, receives the longest message. Known for its trade guilds, the city demanded social conformity. Membership required attendance at pagan feasts where meat was sacrificed to idols and sexual immorality was common. For many Christians, economic survival seemed impossible without compromise. Christ introduces himself as "the Son of God, whose eyes are like a flame of fire, and whose feet are like burnished bronze." His penetrating gaze and unshakable strength reveal that nothing escapes his notice.

The church's report card seems encouraging: love, faith, service, endurance—their works had even increased. Yet love without discernment can invite disaster. A woman symbolically named "Jezebel" (after the idolatrous queen of Israel) taught believers to tolerate sin in the name of spiritual freedom. Perhaps she claimed deeper knowledge, suggesting that participation in guild feasts was a harmless accommodation. Christ's patience had limits: "I gave her time to repent, but she refuses." Judgment would come upon her and those who followed her influence.

For the faithful minority, however, Christ's words breathe assurance: "Hold fast what you have until I come." Perseverance, not perfection, marks the conqueror. To such he grants "authority over the nations" and "the morning star." The promise echoes Psalm 2—believers will share Christ's victory and reign with him in the age to come. The "morning star," a title Christ claims for himself in Revelation 22:16, represents the dawn of eternal fellowship. Thyatira proves that tolerance of falsehood, however compassionate it appears, endangers the soul.

Christ's ongoing call to the church

These four letters display the full spectrum of church life—orthodox yet loveless Ephesus, suffering Smyrna, compromised Pergamum, and tolerant Thyatira. They remind believers that every congregation stands under Christ's inspection. He knows our works, motives, and endurance. He commends, corrects, and commands repentance with perfect balance of justice and grace. The repetition of "He who has an ear, let him hear what the Spirit says to the churches" underscores that these words are timeless.

Revelation's message is not escapist; it is exhortational. The Lord calls his people to fearless faithfulness in a world that alternately threatens and tempts. The rewards—tree of life, crown of life, hidden manna, white stone, authority, morning star—symbolize complete restoration and union with Christ. The conqueror is not the militant, but the steadfast believer who clings to faith through love, suffering, purity, and truth.

For John's readers—and for us—the letters confront every false measure of success. Christ seeks not impressive structures or social approval but hearts aflame with love, courage under pressure, moral clarity, and unwavering devotion. The lampstands still burn because the Lord of the church still walks among them, refining his people for victory.

APPLICATION

1. Love must remain the heart of faith

The Ephesian church reminds us that truth without love becomes lifeless. They were strong defenders of doctrine but weak in devotion. A congregation can win every theological debate or doctrinal argument and still lose the warmth of Christlike affection. The Christian life begins in love—God's love for us and our love in return—and that affection must continually renew every act of service and sacrifice. Without love, ministry becomes maintenance, service becomes selfish, and worship becomes routine. To recover it, Christ calls us to remember what once stirred our hearts, repent of coldness, and repeat the works born of gratitude. When love rules our hearts again, obedience becomes joyful, not burdensome. Every generation must fight the slow drift from affection to apathy, guarding against the subtle danger of doing all the right things for all the wrong reasons.

2. Suffering refines our faith and reveals our riches

Smyrna's story teaches that hardship is not a mark of God's absence but of his nearness. These believers were poor in possessions but rich in faith. Their faithfulness amid loss revealed the reality of their treasure in heaven. Modern Christians often equate blessing with comfort, yet Christ measures wealth differently. The persecuted believer is not impoverished but purified. Every trial is an opportunity to testify that our hope lies beyond what the world can touch. "Be faithful unto death," Christ says, and life will follow. Suffering, though temporary, exposes what truly endures. When faith is tested by pressure, it shines with undiluted devotion. Instead of asking, "Why me?" we learn to ask, "How can this trial glorify Christ?" The crown of life still waits for those who choose faithfulness over fear.

3. Compromise corrodes our witness

Pergamum's compromise began not with rebellion but with small concessions. Believers tolerated what they should have rejected and rationalized what they should have repented of. The lure of social acceptance and economic survival tempted them to blend faith with idolatry. That same danger remains today when Christians try to make peace with sin or silence conviction to avoid offense. Christ's sharp sword reminds us that his word must remain our standard. Purity of heart and truth of doctrine are not luxuries but necessities. To the faithful he promises "hidden manna"—spiritual nourishment—and "a white stone," the token of divine approval. When the world offers comfort at the price of compromise, believers must remember that Christ alone satisfies. The church's influence flows not from imitation of culture but from distinctness within it.

4. Tolerance is not always virtue

Thyatira's believers were known for love, yet they confused compassion with concession. Their tolerance of "Jezebel" revealed a failure to discern. The Lord who sees with eyes like fire calls his people to holiness. Love that refuses correction is not love at all; it is indifference wearing the mask of kindness. Every generation faces the temptation to reshape moral standards to fit the times. But Christ's church must hold fast to truth even when labeled narrow or judgmental. The promise to the overcomer—authority and the morning star—reminds us that holiness always leads to honor. The one who refuses the world's moral darkness will share the light of Christ's eternal dawn. In an age obsessed with acceptance, the church must learn again that fidelity to truth is the deepest form of love.

CONCLUSION

Christ's letters to the churches remind us that he still walks among his people. He knows our works, our motives, and our challenges. To Ephesus, he calls for renewed love; to Smyrna, endurance through suffering; to Pergamum, courage against compromise; and to Thyatira, holiness without apology. These are not ancient messages preserved in stone but living words that search the heart of every congregation today. The one who died and lives forever speaks to us with the same authority and tenderness. If we listen and overcome, his promises become ours—the tree of life, the crown of life, hidden manna, and the morning star. The risen Christ still refines his church until her light shines undimmed in his presence.

REFLECTION

1. What does it mean for a church to lose its first love while maintaining correct doctrine?

2. How does Smyrna's endurance redefine what it means to be spiritually rich?

3. Where do you see the temptation to compromise with the world in modern Christianity?

4. Why does Christ commend discernment as well as love in Thyatira's example?

5. How do the promises to "the one who conquers" motivate you personally to endure?

6. What habits can help believers balance conviction and compassion in daily discipleship?

DISCUSSION

1. Which of the four churches most resembles challenges your congregation faces today?

2. How can Christians rekindle genuine love for Christ that fuels both obedience and joy?

3. What kinds of suffering or social pressure threaten Christians' courage in your setting?

4. How can churches show mercy without tolerating sin or watering down truth?

5. Why is false teaching so spiritually dangerous, even when it sounds appealing?

6. What would it look like for our church to "hold fast" until Christ returns?

4

LETTERS TO THE CHURCHES, PT. 2
REVELATION 3

Objective: To encourage believers to reject complacency, endure faithfully, and depend fully on Christ's sustaining grace.

INTRODUCTION

In 1912, an iceberg sank the Titanic—not because no one saw it, but because those who did refused to believe it could cause harm. Overconfidence dulled their vigilance, and by the time they realized the danger, it was too late. What destroyed that ship was not the ice itself, but the crew's complacency.

That same danger threatens the church. Revelation 3 introduces us to three congregations—Sardis, Philadelphia, and Laodicea—each facing unique tests. Sardis had reputation without reality, Philadelphia had weakness without fear, and Laodicea had wealth without awareness. Christ's words pierce through appearances, revealing what lies beneath the surface. He awakens the complacent, encourages the faithful, and warns the self-satisfied.

These letters remind Christians that the Lord still inspects his people. He looks beyond programs, reputation, and comfort to measure the heart's devotion. Through his rebuke and promise, Jesus calls every church to spiritual alertness, humble endurance, and renewed dependence on him.

EXAMINATION

Christ's continuing message to his churches

The risen Christ's words to the seven churches reveal a Lord who not only reigns above but walks among his people. Revelation 2 introduced the first four congregations—each tested by love, suffering, compromise, or tolerance. Revelation 3 concludes the series with three more: Sardis, Philadelphia, and Laodicea. Together, they complete the portrait of Christ's church in every age. He sees through appearances, encourages endurance, and calls his people to repentance. Each letter begins with an image from the vision in chapter 1, reminding us that the one who speaks is the same Lord whose eyes are like fire and whose voice resounds like many waters. These letters are not relics of the past; they remain Christ's living assessment of his church today.

The church that appeared alive but was dead (3:1–6)

Sardis was an ancient and proud city, perched on a steep hill and considered nearly invincible. Twice in its history, enemies captured it by surprise—once under Cyrus the Great and again under Antiochus—because its guards grew careless. That reputation of overconfidence fits perfectly with the spiritual state of its church. Christ's words are blunt: "You have the reputation of being alive, but you are dead." Outwardly, the congregation seemed vibrant, perhaps known for activity and respectability. But inwardly, its heart had stopped beating. There was motion without life, form without power.

Christ identifies himself as the one who possesses "the seven spirits of God and the seven stars," symbols of divine fullness and authority. The Spirit gives life, but this church had quenched him. The command comes urgently: "Wake up, and strengthen what remains and is about to die." Like soldiers asleep at their post, they must shake off complacency and return to watchfulness. The Lord's warning—"If you will not wake up, I will come like a thief"—recalls both Sardis's humiliating history and Jesus' teaching in the Gospels. His coming in judgment will surprise the unprepared.

Yet hope remains. A few in Sardis "have not soiled their garments," meaning they have remained faithful and morally pure in a corrupt environment. They will "walk with me in white," a symbol of victory and holiness. Christ promises that those who overcome will be clothed in white garments, their names secure in the book of life, and acknowledged before the Father and angels. The message is sobering: reputation means nothing without reality. The living Lord seeks living faith.

The church that kept the faith despite weakness (3:7-13)

In contrast to Sardis's dead orthodoxy, the church in Philadelphia radiated humble faithfulness. The smallest and least influential of the seven cities receives some of the Lord's most tender praise. Christ introduces himself as "the holy one, the true one, who has the key of David, who opens and no one will shut, who shuts and no one opens." This language, drawn from Isaiah 22:22, portrays absolute authority. Christ alone grants access to God's kingdom.

Philadelphia was built on unstable ground and frequently shaken by earthquakes. Many residents lived outside the city walls for safety. That sense of fragility mirrored the congregation's earthly condition. "I know that you have but little power," Jesus says, "and yet you have kept my word and have not denied my name." Weakness did not disqualify them—it magnified grace. Where Sardis had strength without life, Philadelphia had life despite weakness.

Christ promises them "an open door," likely representing opportunity for continued witness. No opposition, whether Jewish hostility or Roman persecution, could close it. Their endurance would vindicate them: "I will make those of the synagogue of Satan…come and bow down before your feet, and they will learn that I have loved you." This is not about vengeance but vindication—the world will one day see that Christ's affection rests on his faithful people.

Then comes a promise of protection: "Because you have kept my word about patient endurance, I will keep you from the hour of trial that is coming on the whole world." This does not imply removal from tribulation but preservation through it—the same kind of spiritual safeguarding Jesus prayed for in John 17:15. Finally, the Lord assures them of permanence: "The one who conquers, I will make him a pillar in the temple of my God." In a city where walls often crumbled, that image carried special comfort. They would never be shaken again. The names written upon them—of God, of the city, and of Christ himself—declare permanent belonging.

Philadelphia shows that spiritual stability comes not from strength but from steadfastness. A small, faithful church can display the greatness of God more vividly than the largest or loudest assembly.

The church that grew lukewarm (3:14–22)

If Philadelphia was weak yet faithful, Laodicea was wealthy yet barren. Located at the intersection of major trade routes, the city was famous for its banking industry, black wool garments, and medical school known for its eye salve. When an earthquake destroyed it in AD 60, Laodicea rebuilt itself without Roman assistance—an act of civic pride that mirrored its church's spiritual posture. Christ's diagnosis is devastating: "You are neither cold nor hot. Would that you were either cold or hot! So, because you are lukewarm…I will spit you out of my mouth."

The metaphor would have been immediately understood. Nearby Hierapolis was known for its hot springs, Colossae for its cool, refreshing water—but Laodicea's aqueduct delivered tepid, mineral-heavy water, unpleasant to taste. The church mirrored its water supply: self-satisfied, unrefreshing, useless. They boasted, "I am rich, I have prospered, and I need nothing," yet Christ saw the truth: "You are wretched, pitiable, poor, blind, and naked." Their material prosperity had blinded them to their spiritual poverty.

Still, Christ's rebuke comes from love. "Those whom I love, I reprove and discipline, so be zealous and repent." The language of affection softens the tone of warning. He counsels them to "buy from me gold refined by fire," true spiritual wealth; "white garments," genuine righteousness; and "salve to anoint your eyes," renewed spiritual vision. Each item contrasts with the city's own pride—their banks, textile industry, and medical expertise. The Lord exposes their illusions to awaken repentance.

Then comes one of Scripture's most personal invitations: "Behold, I stand at the door and knock. If anyone hears my voice and opens the door, I will come in and eat with him, and he with me." Fellowship with Christ is not corporate or automatic—it is individual and intimate. Even a complacent church can open the door again. To the conquerors, Christ promises the highest reward: "I will grant him to sit with me on my throne." The one who once sat complacently on earthly wealth may one day share the throne of the Lamb.

The ongoing relevance of Christ's message

Each of these three letters reveals a danger and a hope that transcend the first century. Sardis warns against spiritual complacency—a faith that coasts on reputation. Philadelphia reminds believers that endurance in weakness honors Christ more than power or prestige. Laodicea exposes the deceit of self-sufficiency and calls for renewed dependence on grace. Together, they form a mirror for the modern church.

Christ's voice in Revelation 3 still pierces every congregation. He walks among us, measuring our vitality not by activity or appearance but by devotion. He delights in faithful endurance more than impressive performance. He disciplines those he loves and opens fellowship to any who will repent and receive him anew.

The Lord who holds the key of David controls every door—of opportunity, deliverance, and judgment. His people are safe not because they are strong but because he is sovereign. Those who hear and heed his call will find what every heart longs for: fellowship with Christ now and unshakable glory in his presence forever.

APPLICATION

1. Guard against the danger of complacency

The church at Sardis teaches that a good reputation can hide a dying soul. They looked alive but were spiritually asleep. Activity and noise can disguise decline, and busyness can replace genuine faith. Complacency always begins quietly—when prayer wanes, when repentance feels unnecessary, when yesterday's victories seem enough for today. Christ's command to "wake up" reminds every believer that spiritual vitality must be renewed daily. We cannot live on memories or momentum; life comes only through the Spirit. Churches and Christians alike must examine themselves: are we alive in the eyes of Christ, or merely respected by others? True revival begins when the people of God recognize their need and strengthen what remains. The Lord of Sardis still calls his people to awaken from comfort and return to watchful devotion.

2. Faithfulness matters more than strength

Philadelphia was weak by worldly standards, yet Christ saw it as strong in faith. Their endurance became their testimony. The Lord delights in believers who cling to his word when they have little else to hold. In a culture that prizes influence, success, and numbers, this church reminds us that faithfulness is the true measure of strength. Christ holds the key of David; he alone opens and closes doors. When opportunities arise or trials persist, we rest in his authority. Endurance is not glamorous, but it is precious to God. Our weakness becomes the stage for his power, and our patience becomes the proof of our love. To the weary Christian who feels unseen, Christ says, "I know that you have kept my word." He turns small faithfulness into eternal honor.

3. Wealth cannot replace spiritual vision

Laodicea's wealth blinded it to its poverty. The Christians there had confused material success with spiritual health. Prosperity can make us self-reliant, dulling our dependence on grace. Christ's rebuke still cuts deep: "You say, 'I need nothing,' not realizing you are poor and blind." Comfort can breed apathy faster than hardship. The cure is repentance fueled by humility. Christ urges his people to "buy from me gold refined by fire"—to trade self-sufficiency for purity, pride for repentance, and complacency for zeal. His loving discipline awakens spiritual sight. When Christians once again see their need, they discover that Christ still stands at the door, knocking. He wants not ritual acknowledgment but fellowship. Spiritual renewal begins when we open the door and let him restore the warmth that wealth and ease have smothered.

4. Christ's love always invites renewal

Every rebuke in Revelation 3 flows from love. "Those whom I love, I reprove and discipline." Even Laodicea's harshest correction carries the tenderness of a Savior who refuses to give up on his people. His knock is patient, his call personal, and his promise intimate: "I will come in and eat with him." No matter how far believers drift, Christ desires restored fellowship. That truth changes how we view discipline—not as rejection, but as rescue. He confronts our complacency to reclaim our hearts. The final promise of this chapter is breathtaking: those who overcome will sit with Christ on his throne. The same grace that exposes our failures also exalts the faithful. The Lord's correction, when received humbly, becomes the doorway to deeper communion and everlasting glory.

CONCLUSION

The last three churches in Revelation remind us that Christ's evaluation always reaches the heart. Sardis warns us that spiritual activity without vitality leads to death. Philadelphia proves that steadfast faith in weakness brings honor. Laodicea reveals that comfort and wealth can conceal spiritual blindness. Through every word, Christ calls his people to wake up, hold fast, and open the door once again to his fellowship. His correction is never cruel—it is the expression of love that refuses to leave his church unchanged. Those who respond in repentance and endurance will share his victory, sitting with him on his throne. The risen Lord still walks among his lampstands, refining his people for eternal glory.

REFLECTION

1. What spiritual dangers does Sardis reveal about relying on reputation instead of reality?

2. How can a small or struggling congregation demonstrate the strength of Philadelphia's faithfulness?

3. In what ways can wealth or comfort dull a believer's awareness of spiritual need?

4. Why does Christ discipline those he loves, and how does that truth change repentance?

5. What does the image of Christ knocking at the door teach about his patience and mercy?

6. How do the promises to those who overcome shape your view of perseverance?

DISCUSSION

1. How can Christians today "wake up" and strengthen what remains before faith grows cold?

2. What does it mean for a church to have "an open door" that no one can shut?

3. How might modern believers guard against self-sufficiency and rediscover dependence on grace?

4. What steps can help a congregation listen to Christ's rebuke without becoming discouraged?

5. Why is it difficult for affluent Christians to recognize their spiritual poverty?

6. How can the promise of sharing Christ's throne inspire faithfulness in daily life?

5

THE THRONE & THE LAMB
REVELATION 4-5

Objective: To inspire believers to worship faithfully, resisting worldly power through allegiance to the sovereign Lamb.

INTRODUCTION

In 1936, as Nazi banners draped the streets of Berlin for the Olympics, the world watched a display of power, order, and national pride. Yet in a small house church somewhere in Germany, believers gathered quietly to sing hymns about another kingdom—one not built on violence or fear, but on grace. Their worship was more than devotion; it was defiance. It declared that Christ, not Hitler, was Lord.

That same act of resistance lies at the heart of Revelation 4-5. John's vision pulls back the curtain on the true center of authority in the universe. While Rome paraded its power and demanded allegiance, heaven revealed a throne higher than Caesar's and a ruler greater than any emperor. Around that throne, creation and redemption unite in worship.

Before the church faces the beasts of persecution and deception, John wants them to see this: the universe is not ruled by chaos or cruelty but by a slain Lamb. The power that saves is the power that serves, and worship becomes the Christian's declaration of loyalty to the only one who is worthy.

EXAMINATION

A door opened in heaven (4:1-2)

After the seven messages to the churches, John is invited to see what lies beyond the ordinary. "After this I looked, and behold, a door standing open in heaven!" What follows is not a change of location but of perspective. Heaven's open door allows John—and the churches he represents—to see reality as it truly is. The vision begins not with beasts or battles, but with a throne. Everything in Revelation flows from this image. Before the scrolls are opened, before judgments unfold, before the dragon rages, the church must first see that God reigns.

The "voice like a trumpet" is the same that called John in chapter 1, reminding us that the heavenly and earthly scenes belong together. When John says he was "in the Spirit," it signals a prophetic vision similar to Ezekiel's (Ezek. 1). He is granted insight into the unseen world so that the churches may interpret their own world rightly. What they see on earth—Rome's power, persecution, or chaos—must be redefined by what John sees in heaven: the throne of God, unmoved and unthreatened.

The one seated on the throne (4:3-6a)

John struggles for words. The one seated on the throne appears like "jasper and carnelian," radiant colors of majesty and purity. An emerald rainbow encircles the throne—a sign that divine power is bound by mercy, recalling God's covenant with Noah. Lightning, thunder, and fire evoke Sinai's holiness. The seven torches of fire before the throne represent the fullness of the Spirit, connecting divine transcendence with divine presence.

The sea of glass "like crystal" lies before the throne, calm and untroubled. In the ancient world, the sea symbolized chaos and evil, but here it is perfectly still under God's authority. What terrifies humanity is transparent and subdued before him. The vision establishes the central truth of Revelation: before human thrones and beasts of power appear, there is already a throne that rules all. God's sovereignty is not future—it is now.

This heavenly throne room is not meant to depict the architecture of heaven but to form the theology of worship. John shows the churches who truly reigns. The emperor might boast of dominion and divine favor, but heaven's scene exposes his fraud. The church is invited to lift its eyes above Rome's marble halls to the true center of the universe.

The worship of creation (4:6b-11)

Around the throne are four living creatures—reminiscent of Ezekiel's cherubim—each representing aspects of creation: the lion (wild beasts), the ox (domestic animals), the man (humanity), and the eagle (birds of the air). They are full of eyes, alert to the glory of God, and they never cease to declare, "Holy, holy, holy, is the Lord God Almighty, who was and is and is to come!" All creation worships its Maker.

Surrounding them are twenty-four elders, symbolizing the unified people of God—the twelve tribes of Israel and the twelve apostles. They wear white robes and golden crowns, tokens of victory and priesthood. When the living creatures praise, the elders fall down, casting their crowns before the throne. Authority and achievement are surrendered in worship. Their song interprets creation's meaning: "Worthy are you, our Lord and God, to receive glory and honor and power, for you created all things."

This language directly challenges Roman imperial worship. The emperor Domitian had demanded to be addressed as "Our Lord and God." John's audience would recognize the subversive irony: only the Creator deserves that title. The scene reorients the church's loyalty and imagination. Worship becomes resistance—an act of allegiance to the true King.

This is dissident discipleship. The church's first political act is doxology. In singing to the Creator, believers reject every false lord who demands devotion. Revelation 4 is not escapist mysticism; it is prophetic realism. When the church gathers around the throne in worship, it declares that the Lamb's kingdom is the only lasting one.

The sealed scroll and the search for worthiness (5:1-4)

John's gaze shifts from the throne to the right hand of the one who sits upon it. There he sees a scroll written on both sides and sealed with seven seals. It represents God's redemptive plan—his purpose for history, justice, and salvation. Yet no one in heaven or on earth can open it or even look into it. John weeps, not because he is curious, but because if no one can open the scroll, history remains locked; evil goes unchallenged, and God's promises seem delayed.

His grief captures the church's longing: Who will bring justice? Who will make sense of our suffering? Who will unveil the story God is writing? The silence of heaven reveals the limits of all earthly power. No emperor, prophet, or angel can execute God's purposes. Redemption cannot be accomplished by force or intellect—it must come through worthiness.

The Lion who is the Lamb (5:5–10)

One of the elders interrupts John's tears: "Weep no more; behold, the Lion of the tribe of Judah, the Root of David, has conquered." Expectation builds—surely a mighty warrior approaches. But when John turns, he does not see a lion. He sees "a Lamb standing, as though it had been slain." The two images fuse into one: Christ conquers not through violence but through sacrifice. The cross is heaven's definition of victory.

The Lamb's seven horns symbolize perfect power, his seven eyes the fullness of the Spirit sent into all the earth. He approaches the throne and takes the scroll—the act of supreme authority. At that moment, heaven erupts. The living creatures and elders fall down before the Lamb, holding golden bowls of incense, "which are the prayers of the saints." The prayers of the persecuted have not been forgotten; they become the fragrance of worship before God.

Their song declares the gospel in miniature: "Worthy are you to take the scroll and to open its seals, for you were slain, and by your blood you ransomed people for God from every tribe and language and people and nation." The Lamb's victory unites the nations into one kingdom and priesthood. His blood achieves what no empire could—reconciliation without domination. In a world obsessed with conquest, Revelation 5 proclaims redemption through cruciform power.

The worship of the redeemed (5:11–14)

The circle of worship widens. Myriads of angels join the chorus, their voices numbering "ten thousand times ten thousand." The universe vibrates with praise: "Worthy is the Lamb who was slain, to receive power and wealth and wisdom and might and honor and glory and blessing!" Each word of praise ascribes to the Lamb what the empire claimed for Caesar. The worship of heaven is the resistance of earth.

Then all creation joins in: "To him who sits on the throne and to the Lamb be blessing and honor and glory and might forever and ever!" The scene ends where it began—with God's sovereignty—but now the Lamb shares that throne. The Creator and Redeemer reign together. Creation's purpose and redemption's goal converge in one eternal song.

For the suffering churches of Asia, this vision was not abstract theology; it was survival. When the emperor demanded allegiance, when trade guilds required participation in pagan feasts, when faithfulness meant poverty or death, this vision reminded them who truly held the future. To worship the Lamb was to resist the beast; to sing the songs of heaven was to defy the propaganda of empire.

The throne and the Lamb as the center of reality

Revelation 4–5 are not merely a prelude to the judgments that follow—they are the interpretive key to the entire book. Before the seals, trumpets, or bowls appear, John shows us what is ultimate. The universe is not chaotic but ordered around a throne and a Lamb. The power structures of the world—political, military, or economic—are temporary imitations of this eternal authority.

John's vision forms a counter-narrative to empire. Rome's throne projected power through fear; God's throne radiates holiness through love. Rome demanded worship enforced by violence; the Lamb invites worship through sacrifice. The Lamb's kingdom grows not by the sword but by the Spirit.

For Christians, the invitation is clear: come and see what heaven sees. Worship redefines reality. When Christians gather to pray, sing, and break bread, they participate in this heavenly drama. Each act of faithful worship is a protest against idolatry, a pledge of allegiance to the Lamb, and a reminder that our citizenship belongs to a kingdom not made by hands.

From vision to vocation

John's readers were ordinary believers living in the shadow of empire, but Revelation 4–5 lifts them into a new vocation—to live as priests and kings serving the Lamb. Their resistance is not rebellion but worship; their endurance is not despair but faith. The throne and the Lamb remind them that the church's mission is not to seize control but to bear witness, not to mirror Rome's power but to reflect the Lamb's humility.

In every generation, the church must recover this heavenly vision. When we lose sight of the throne, we begin to fear the empires of earth.

When we forget the Lamb, we start to imitate the beasts. But when our worship is shaped by this vision—holy, humble, and hopeful—we find strength to persevere and courage to stand apart. The throne defines what is real; the Lamb defines what is worthy.

APPLICATION

1. Worship redefines reality

John's vision begins not with chaos on earth but with peace in heaven. The throne scene reminds believers that worship is not escape—it is resistance. When we gather to praise the Creator and the Lamb, we are declaring that God, not empire, rules the world. The early Christians who first heard Revelation lived under Rome's propaganda, yet their songs told a different story. The same is true today. In a world that worships success, security, and power, worship recenters us on what is ultimate. It pulls our attention from the noise of politics and possessions to the holiness of God. Every prayer, hymn, and act of obedience becomes a confession: "You are worthy." Worship is the church's act of protest against idolatry and her confession of loyalty to the Lamb who reigns.

2. Power is redefined by the cross

When John heard of a Lion, he turned and saw a Lamb. That reversal changes everything. The Lion conquers not by devouring enemies but by dying for them. In Christ's kingdom, victory comes through vulnerability, and power is measured by love. This vision challenges every instinct to dominate or control. The Lamb's followers win the same way he did—through faithfulness, truth, and sacrificial service. The church's mission, therefore, is not to seize cultural influence but to embody cruciform love. This is dissident discipleship—living in such a way that the Lamb's nonviolent, self-giving rule defines our lives. In a world obsessed with triumph, the gospel invites us to a different kind of conquest: to overcome evil with good, fear with faith, and hatred with love.

3. Prayer and worship join heaven and earth

Before the Lamb are "golden bowls full of incense, which are the prayers of the saints." Our prayers participate in the drama of heaven. Every whispered plea, every cry for justice, every song of gratitude ascends before the throne. The persecuted believers of John's day might have felt unheard, but Revelation 5 shows otherwise—their prayers fill heaven's temple. God's response to the world's brokenness begins with the prayers of his people. This vision should deepen our confidence in prayer and renew our reverence in worship. When Christians gather, we are not spectators at a service but participants in the worship of heaven. Our voices join those of angels and elders declaring that the Lamb is worthy. Worship is not background music to faith; it is the heartbeat of resistance and the lifeblood of hope.

4. The Lamb's victory shapes our allegiance

Revelation 4–5 confronts every rival loyalty. Rome demanded citizens to proclaim, "Caesar is Lord." John's readers refused because they had already confessed, "Jesus is Lord." Allegiance to the Lamb requires rejecting the idols of empire—whether political, national, or personal—that promise safety in exchange for devotion. The Lamb alone is worthy of total trust. This calls believers to evaluate where their true loyalty lies: Do our choices, words, and priorities reflect the reign of Christ or the values of empire? To follow the Lamb is to adopt his posture of humility and his pattern of sacrifice. The redeemed people of God live as witnesses to a different kind of kingdom—one built not on fear but on faith, not on coercion but on compassion. True discipleship means our allegiance belongs to the throne and the Lamb alone.

CONCLUSION

Revelation 4–5 shows the church where true power lies. Before the scrolls are opened and judgments unfold, John is given a vision of heaven's center—a throne occupied by the Creator and a Lamb who was slain yet lives. This vision anchors believers in every age. Empires rise and fall, but the Lamb remains enthroned. His kingdom advances not through coercion but through sacrificial love. Worship, then, is not escape from the world's troubles but allegiance to its true King. The church's song, "Worthy is the Lamb," becomes both comfort and calling. It reminds us that every act of faithful endurance joins the chorus of heaven, proclaiming that the crucified Christ reigns forever.

REFLECTION

1. How does John's vision of the throne challenge the way you see power and control?

2. What does the contrast between the Lion and the Lamb reveal about the nature of Christ's victory?

3. In what ways does worship serve as an act of resistance against worldly idols?

4. How do the prayers of the saints before the throne encourage you to persevere in faith?

5. What images or phrases in Revelation 4–5 most expand your understanding of God's glory?

6. How does seeing the Lamb on the throne strengthen your trust when the world feels chaotic?

DISCUSSION

1. What might modern "empires" look like, and how can Christians resist their influence?

2. Why do you think Revelation portrays heaven's response to evil as worship rather than warfare?

3. How does this vision redefine the meaning of victory for believers today?

4. What can churches learn from the elders and creatures who continually praise God?

5. How does this passage help us view prayer and worship as participation in heaven's mission?

6. What would it look like for your congregation to live with its allegiance fully centered on the Lamb?

6

THE SEALS & THE REDEEMED
REVELATION 6-7

Objective: To strengthen believers' confidence in Christ's sovereignty and sealing amid the world's suffering and uncertainty.

INTRODUCTION

In 1941, as bombs fell over London, Winston Churchill visited the smoldering ruins of St. Paul's Cathedral. Though much of the city lay in rubble, the cathedral's great dome still stood, rising through the smoke. For many, that image became a symbol of endurance—proof that even in devastation, something greater remained unshaken.

That same message echoes through Revelation 6-7. As the Lamb opens the seals, the world appears to crumble under conquest, war, famine, and death. Yet above the noise, heaven's throne stands firm, and the redeemed of God remain secure. The vision confronts Christians with hard truth: the church's path runs through suffering, not around it. But it also offers deep assurance: the Lamb reigns, and his people are sealed.

John's vision answers the question, "Who can stand?" with a confident reply—those who belong to the Lamb. Their security is not found in comfort or control, but in God's mark upon them and his promise to bring them safely through the storm.

EXAMINATION

The Lamb who opens the seals (6:1-2)

When the door to heaven opened in chapters 4-5, John saw the throne and the Lamb. Now the Lamb begins to open the scroll that only he was found worthy to take. What unfolds is not a chronological prediction of end-time disasters but a symbolic revelation of the church's experience throughout history. The Lamb reigns, and what follows occurs under his authority. The world's pain is neither random nor outside divine control.

As the first seal opens, John sees a white horse. Its rider carries a bow and goes out "conquering, and to conquer." Interpreters have long debated his identity, but in context this horse symbolizes the human lust for domination—the conquest that drives nations and empires. Though the color white can suggest victory or righteousness, this rider's mission is conquest through force, not redemption. The Lamb allows such forces to ride forth, but they remain under his sovereignty. The church is not called to join these riders but to endure amid them.

War, scarcity, and death (6:3-8)

The second, third, and fourth seals release the next three horsemen—red, black, and pale. Together they represent the recurring sorrows of human history: war, economic oppression, and death. The red horse brings violence, taking peace from the earth. The black horse carries scales, symbolizing famine and economic imbalance—"a quart of wheat for a denarius," a day's wage for a day's food, while the wealthy remain untouched. The pale horse (more accurately a puke green color) brings death and Hades, claiming a fourth of the earth.

John's readers would have recognized these as familiar realities, not future predictions. The horsemen gallop across every century, reminding believers that the world's suffering is not evidence of Christ's absence but proof of his patience. History's tragedies are permitted, not uncontrolled. The Lamb's sovereignty means that evil is temporary and never ultimate. These seals pull back the curtain on human violence and greed, exposing the brokenness of a world estranged from its Creator.

For believers, the message is sobering but hopeful. The church's endurance must not depend on political peace or economic stability. Even when the world unravels, the Lamb still opens the seals.

The cry of the martyrs (6:9-11)

The fifth seal shifts the scene from earth's chaos to heaven's altar. John sees "the souls of those who had been slain for the word of God." These are not ghosts but living witnesses, faithful even unto death. Their cry—"How long, O Lord?"—echoes the laments of the Psalms and prophets. They do not seek revenge but righteous vindication. Their longing is for God to finish what he has promised, to bring justice and reveal his holiness to the world.

Each is given a white robe, symbolizing purity and honor, and told to "rest a little longer." God's timing is deliberate; his plan includes others yet to suffer for his name. The martyrs' rest is not neglect but assurance—justice will come, but on heaven's schedule. Their voices remind the church that lament is a form of faith. To cry "How long?" is to trust that God hears and will act. The blood of the saints, unseen by the world, becomes the seed of endurance for the generations that follow.

The great day of wrath (6:12-17)

The sixth seal unveils cosmic upheaval—earthquakes, darkened skies, falling stars, and a trembling creation. These images echo the prophets (Isa. 13; Joel 2) and symbolize the collapse of earthly powers under divine judgment. Kings, generals, rich and poor alike hide in terror, crying out for the mountains to fall on them. The question rings through the chaos: "Who can stand?"

This question becomes the hinge between chapters 6 and 7. God's wrath reveals the fragility of human kingdoms and exposes the illusion of security. The church, however, is not called to fear but to trust. The same Lord who shakes the heavens seals his people for preservation. Judgment and mercy are two sides of the same sovereignty.

The sealing of God's servants (7:1-8)

Before the seventh seal is opened, there is a pause—a divine interlude of protection. Four angels hold back the winds of destruction until the servants of God are sealed on their foreheads. The seal represents ownership, identity, and preservation. In the ancient world, seals marked what belonged to a ruler. Here, believers are marked as God's own possession, just as Israel's doorposts bore blood during the Passover.

John hears the number of the sealed—144,000, twelve thousand from each tribe of Israel. This is not a literal census but a symbolic image of completeness. Twelve (the number of God's covenant people) squared and multiplied by a thousand (the number of vastness and perfection) represents the totality of the redeemed. The exclusion of the tribe of Dan, traditionally associated with idolatry, underscores the purity of this spiritual Israel.

To John's readers, surrounded by the might of Rome, the sealing assured them that nothing—not persecution, famine, or death—could erase their belonging to God. The seal does not spare them from suffering; it preserves them through it. Their security lies not in escape from tribulation but in endurance within it.

The great multitude before the throne (7:9–17)

After hearing the number, John turns and sees—and what he sees transcends what he heard. "A great multitude that no one could number, from every nation, from all tribes and peoples and languages, standing before the throne and before the Lamb." The 144,000 and the multitude are the same group viewed from two perspectives: the church militant on earth and the church triumphant in glory.

Their white robes signify righteousness, and their palm branches recall Israel's festivals of victory and peace. Their song answers the question of 6:17: "Who can stand?"—those redeemed by the Lamb. "Salvation belongs to our God who sits on the throne, and to the Lamb!" The angels, elders, and living creatures respond in unison, amplifying the chorus of heaven.

When one of the elders explains the vision, he identifies the multitude as "those who have come out of the great tribulation." This phrase describes not a future seven-year period but the ongoing struggle of the church in a hostile world. Christians conquer by perseverance, not escape. Their robes are washed in the blood of the Lamb—a paradox of purity through sacrifice.

The vision closes with tenderness: the redeemed serve God "day and night in his temple," sheltered by his presence. Hunger, thirst, and scorching heat are gone. The Lamb becomes their shepherd, leading them to living water, and God wipes away every tear. The suffering of chapter 6 finds its answer here—not in avoidance, but in transformation.

The meaning of the seals and the redeemed

Revelation 6–7 shifts our gaze from fear to faith. The horsemen show that war, famine, and death are not outside Christ's control. The martyrs remind us that suffering does not silence the church but deepens its witness. The sealed and the multitude reveal that redemption is complete and secure. Together, these chapters declare that history is not driven by chaos but governed by the Lamb.

John trains believers to see the world's suffering through the lens of God's sovereignty and to remain faithful when empire threatens or seduces. The Lamb reigns even when the world unravels. To live as his followers is to live in resistance—to refuse despair, violence, or idolatry, and to rest in the promise that the sealed will stand.

Revelation 6–7 answers the cry "How long?" with assurance: the story is not out of control. The Lamb holds the scroll, the saints are sealed, and the redeemed will sing.

APPLICATION

1. Christ's sovereignty steadies the church amid chaos

The opening of the seals reminds us that history's pain unfolds under the Lamb's authority. Conquest, war, famine, and death are not random forces but realities permitted within God's redemptive plan. That truth does not minimize suffering—it anchors faith within it. When the world shakes, Christians must remember who holds the scroll. Empires rise, markets collapse, and violence scars the earth, yet Christ reigns. Revelation teaches us to interpret headlines through heaven's perspective. The Lamb governs what we fear most and sets limits to every evil. Instead of despair, we respond with endurance. Instead of panic, we practice prayer. Our hope is not in escaping hardship but in trusting that the Lamb is already Lord. Every faithful act of endurance becomes a quiet protest against the illusion that chaos rules the world.

2. Lament is faith's language in waiting

The martyrs' cry, "How long, O Lord?" expresses both grief and confidence. Their lament is not doubt but devotion; they speak to God because they trust his justice. In seasons of persecution, loss, or uncertainty, Christians may feel forgotten, yet Revelation shows those voices rising like incense before the throne. Honest lament is an act of faith, not failure. It refuses to accept injustice as final and clings to the hope that God will act. When the church prays this way, it joins the saints beneath the altar and anticipates the day when every wrong will be made right. We are not called to silence our sorrow but to sanctify it—to let our tears testify that we believe God's kingdom will come. The cry of "How long?" keeps faith alive until the Lamb wipes every tear away.

3. God's seal secures our identity, not our comfort

The sealing of the 144,000 teaches that believers are protected spiritually, not insulated physically. God's seal marks ownership and destiny, not exemption from hardship. The church is preserved through tribulation, not removed from it. In a world that values safety above faithfulness, this vision calls Christians to a deeper kind of security—the assurance that nothing can separate us from the love of God. The mark on the believer's forehead contrasts sharply with the mark of the beast that will later appear. The faithful belong to the Lamb; their allegiance cannot be erased by persecution or poverty. To be sealed is to be known, kept, and empowered to endure. When we live as those sealed by God's Spirit, our courage becomes the evidence of his protection, and our endurance becomes the testimony of his reign.

4. The redeemed community embodies hope for the nations

John first *hears* the number—144,000—but then *sees* the multitude no one can count. The same people are described twice: the sealed on earth and the saved in heaven. The church's identity is both militant and triumphant, both suffering and victorious. This vision expands our imagination of who belongs to God's family. From every tribe, language, and nation, the redeemed stand together before the throne. Their unity is not political or cultural but spiritual, formed by the blood of the Lamb. In a divided world, the church embodies the future harmony of God's kingdom. Every act of hospitality, reconciliation, or cross-cultural love becomes a preview of that multitude. Our worship on earth anticipates the worship of heaven, where all nations will sing one song: "Salvation belongs to our God and to the Lamb."

CONCLUSION

Revelation 6–7 assures believers that history is not spiraling out of control. The Lamb who opens the seals governs the chaos, limits evil, and preserves his people through every trial. The horsemen may ride, but the throne still stands. The saints may cry, "How long?" but their prayers rise before God as incense. The church may suffer, but she is sealed for eternity. The multitude in white robes proves that the story ends in victory, not defeat. Every believer who endures bears the mark of divine ownership and the hope of everlasting joy. The one who reigns with wounds in his hands guarantees that suffering will never have the final word.

REFLECTION

1. What does the image of the Lamb opening the seals teach about God's control over history?

2. How does Revelation 6 help you interpret the world's violence and suffering through faith?

3. Why is the martyrs' cry "How long?" an act of trust rather than doubt?

4. What does being "sealed" by God mean for your sense of identity and security?

5. How does the vision of the great multitude shape your hope for the church's future?

6. What comforts you most in knowing that the Lamb is both Redeemer and Ruler?

DISCUSSION

1. How can Christians today resist despair when facing global chaos or personal suffering?

2. In what ways can the church recover lament as a faithful expression of hope?

3. Why is it important that God's people are sealed through tribulation rather than spared from it?

4. What practices can help Christians live with confidence in the Lamb's sovereignty?

5. How does Revelation 7 challenge cultural or national boundaries within the church?

6. What would change in your worship if you saw it as joining the multitude before the throne?

7

TRUMPETS OF JUDGMENT

REVELATION 8-9

Objective: To encourage Christians to trust God's justice and proclaim repentance amid a world under judgment.

INTRODUCTION

In 1883, the volcanic island of Krakatoa exploded with a force so powerful that it was heard three thousand miles away. The blast darkened skies around the world and lowered global temperatures for years. Yet even that staggering event pales beside the imagery of Revelation 8-9. When the trumpets sound, creation itself convulses—mountains burn, rivers turn bitter, the sky grows dark. It is as if God allows the world to feel the weight of its rebellion.

But these judgments are not mindless destruction; they are mercy's last warning. John's vision reminds believers that the chaos of history unfolds under heaven's control. The Lamb has not abdicated his throne. The prayers of the saints still rise, and the trumpet blasts still call the world to repent before it is too late.

Revelation 8-9 reveals a sobering truth: the God who saves also judges. Yet even in wrath, his goal is restoration. The church's task is to pray, endure, and proclaim that behind every shaking of the earth stands a sovereign and merciful Lord who still desires repentance rather than ruin.

EXAMINATION

The silence in heaven (8:1–5)

When the Lamb opens the seventh seal, John expects another burst of noise—lightning, thunder, or worship. Instead, there is silence. "When the Lamb opened the seventh seal, there was silence in heaven for about half an hour." In a book filled with sound, this pause is striking. It is not emptiness but awe. Heaven holds its breath as the prayers of the saints rise like incense before God. The judgments that follow are not random eruptions of chaos but responses to the prayers of the faithful. The silence declares that divine justice proceeds from divine holiness.

An angel stands at the golden altar, holding a censer filled with the saints' prayers and burning incense. He hurls the censer to the earth, and the result is thunder, lightning, and earthquake—the same imagery that surrounded Sinai and the throne of God. In Revelation, prayer moves history. The judgments that follow are God's righteous answer to the cries of those who have suffered injustice. Heaven's stillness precedes earth's shaking.

The sounding of the trumpets (8:6)

The seven angels stand ready, each with a trumpet. In Scripture, trumpets announce divine presence, warn of battle, and call for worship. The fall of Jericho and the plagues of Egypt stand behind John's imagery. Each trumpet announces that the Creator will not ignore creation's corruption. The trumpets do not describe sequential events but recurring realities of divine judgment throughout history—partial, purposeful, and restrained. They expose the fragility of a world built on rebellion and summon humanity to repentance.

The church is not meant to decode timetables but to discern truth: God's judgments interrupt idolatry, reveal sin's consequences, and urge repentance before it's too late. The trumpets are divine wake-up calls.

The first four trumpets: Judgment upon creation (8:7–12)

As the first angel sounds, hail and fire mixed with blood fall upon the earth, echoing the plague upon Egypt (Exod. 9:22–26). A third of the earth, trees, and grass are burned—a symbol of environmental devastation and the breakdown of stability. The second trumpet strikes the sea; a blazing mountain falls into it, turning a third of it to blood. The third trumpet poisons the rivers as "a great star, blazing like a torch," falls from heaven—its name is *Wormwood*, meaning bitterness. The fourth trumpet darkens the sun, moon, and stars, dimming a third of their light.

These judgments are not literal meteorological disasters but symbolic portrayals of the created order unraveling under humanity's sin. The repetition of "a third" emphasizes restraint. God's wrath is real but measured; his goal is repentance, not annihilation. These images also mock the claims of the Roman Empire. Rome boasted that its peace and prosperity reflected divine favor, but John's vision reveals creation itself protesting empire's idolatry. The same creation that once sang "holy, holy, holy" (4:8) now groans under human rebellion.

As the fourth trumpet fades, an eagle cries with a loud voice, "Woe, woe, woe to those who dwell on the earth!" The stage is set for the final three trumpets, which will shift from ecological to spiritual devastation.

The fifth trumpet: Torment from the abyss (9:1-11)

The fifth angel sounds, and a "star fallen from heaven" is given the key to the abyss. This fallen star represents a demonic power—perhaps Satan himself—permitted to unleash destruction but still operating under divine control. When the abyss opens, smoke rises like from a furnace, darkening the air and releasing locusts that torment rather than destroy. These are not ordinary insects but nightmarish symbols of demonic oppression. John's language recalls Joel 2's locust army but now spiritualized into a vision of evil set loose on those "who do not have the seal of God."

The locusts' grotesque description—faces like humans, teeth like lions, wings like chariots—embodies the ugliness of sin and deception. Their power lasts "five months," a normal locust season, emphasizing that their reign is limited. The torment they inflict mirrors the psychological and spiritual misery of life apart from God—despair without death, rebellion without rest. Their king is called Abaddon or Apollyon, "the Destroyer." Yet even destruction serves divine restraint. Evil is neither autonomous nor infinite; it functions within boundaries set by the Lamb.

For the sealed people of God, this judgment is not punishment but protection. Those marked by God endure hardship but are not spiritually destroyed. Revelation 9 teaches that the greatest terror is not physical suffering but separation from God—the self-inflicted torment of idolatry.

The sixth trumpet: War unleashed (9:13–19)

When the sixth angel sounds, four bound angels at the Euphrates are released. In John's world, the Euphrates marked the boundary of Rome's empire and the edge of known civilization. To mention it was to invoke fear of invasion and chaos. Here, it symbolizes God permitting the destructive potential of human sin to run its course. A vast cavalry—two hundred million strong—sweeps across the earth, breathing fire, smoke, and sulfur. These riders are not literal armies but personifications of death and destruction unleashed by humanity's own violence.

The imagery recalls the plagues of Egypt and the prophetic visions of Joel and Jeremiah. As in those texts, the purpose of judgment is to awaken repentance. The terrifying scenes of Revelation 9 are divine warnings, not vindictive punishments. God's justice exposes the futility of a world that trusts in its own power. Every empire that exalts itself eventually becomes the instrument of its own ruin.

Yet even here, God's control remains absolute. The number of those killed is limited to a third. Evil is permitted to wound but not to wipe out. The judgments remind believers that God alone determines history's boundaries.

The tragedy of unrepentant hearts (9:20–21)

The chapter closes with one of Revelation's most tragic lines: "The rest of mankind, who were not killed by these plagues, did not repent." Despite clear warnings, humanity clings to its idols. John lists them—"idols of gold and silver and bronze and stone and wood, which cannot see or hear or walk." Like the psalmist before him, John exposes the irony: worshipers become like the gods they adore—blind, deaf, lifeless.

Their refusal to repent reveals sin's power to harden. They persist in "murders, sorceries, sexual immorality, and thefts." The world's crises do not automatically lead to spiritual awakening; suffering alone cannot produce repentance. Only the Spirit's conviction can soften hearts. For John's audience, this warning underscored the danger of complacency. Rome's prosperity had lulled many into compromise. But the church must not mistake patience for permission. The partial judgments of the trumpets anticipate the final judgment yet offer mercy in the meantime.

The purpose of the trumpets

The trumpet judgments answer the question raised by the martyrs' cry, "How long?" (6:10). God's response comes not through immediate vengeance but through progressive warnings. The trumpets demonstrate that divine justice is both patient and purposeful. God desires repentance, not ruin. His wrath is the flip side of his love—a holy refusal to let evil go unchecked.

Revelation 8–9 also reveals a crucial truth about the nature of evil. The judgments are terrifying, yet they show that evil is self-destructive. Humanity's idolatry unleashes its own torment. The abyss opens, and darkness spreads—but only because people have chosen to reject the light. Still, even these judgments are framed by the prayers of the saints and the sovereignty of the Lamb. The same fire that consumes also purifies; the same thunder that terrifies also vindicates.

Faithful Christians live in a world shaken by God's trumpet blasts yet refuse to join the chorus of rebellion. Their endurance itself becomes a testimony. When creation groans, the church prays. When empire collapses, the church worships. When others curse, the church proclaims that salvation still belongs to the Lamb.

Faithful endurance amid warning and wrath

The church today lives between the silence of heaven and the trumpet of judgment. The visions of Revelation 8–9 are not meant to paralyze believers with fear but to awaken awe, reverence, and repentance. Every trumpet reminds us that time is both a gift and a warning. God's patience is not weakness but mercy; his judgments are not chaos but compassion calling us home.

For those sealed by the Spirit, the message is assurance: no force, demonic or human, operates outside the Lamb's control. The same throne that governs worship in heaven governs the storms on earth. When the world trembles, the church must not echo its panic. Instead, we bear witness to a different kingdom—a kingdom where justice flows from love, power is defined by the cross, and mercy remains available to all who repent.

Revelation 8–9 ends not with finality but with unfinished business. The trumpets have sounded, yet the world remains unrepentant. The church's task is clear: to live as the echo of heaven's silence and the answer to its prayers—to embody the patience, purity, and perseverance of those who believe that the Lamb's mercy still stands before the final blast.

APPLICATION

1. Prayer participates in God's justice

Before any trumpet sounds, the prayers of the saints ascend like incense before God's throne. This imagery reminds believers that prayer is not passive. It is participation in divine purpose. The world may seem unmoved by our petitions, yet heaven falls silent to listen. The judgments that follow are not arbitrary acts of wrath but God's righteous response to the cries of his people. Every plea for justice, every groan for deliverance, becomes part of heaven's liturgy. The church's first weapon against evil is not outrage but intercession. When we pray, we declare that only God can make the world right. Revelation teaches us that prayer shapes history more than empires do. The hands lifted in worship today will help bring about the renewal of creation tomorrow.

2. God's judgments call humanity to repentance

The trumpets are not divine tantrums but divine warnings. Each one echoes with mercy: the destruction is partial, not total—"a third" of creation affected. God's goal is not annihilation but awakening. He shakes the world to rouse hardened hearts. Yet the tragedy of Revelation 9 is that most still refuse to repent. Their idolatry blinds them, turning them into images of their lifeless gods. These passages remind the church that suffering alone cannot convert a soul; only the gospel can. Our mission is to interpret the world's pain through the lens of God's patience, urging repentance while mercy remains open. The church's witness should echo the trumpets—warning, pleading, and pointing to the Lamb whose wounds still invite sinners home.

3. Evil is powerful but never sovereign

The locusts from the abyss and the fiery cavalry from the Euphrates terrify, but they operate under strict limits. The fallen star must be *given* the key;

the demonic hordes can harm only those without God's seal. Evil never acts apart from divine permission. This truth guards believers from fear and despair. Satan may rage, but he is on a leash. The Lamb still holds the scroll. This assurance does not minimize suffering; it magnifies sovereignty. God's people may be wounded, but they are never abandoned. To live faithfully in a hostile world means trusting that every force of darkness is ultimately subordinate to Christ. The demonic powers unleashed in judgment remind the faithful that even hell's fury cannot overcome heaven's authority.

4. Worship is the church's faithful response

The world trembles under judgment, yet the church's response is not terror but trust. While trumpets sound and empires fall, believers worship. Their songs declare that God's holiness is good, his justice right, and his mercy available. Worship lifts our eyes from the fear of destruction to the certainty of redemption. It reminds us that the silence in heaven precedes victory, not defeat. When the world interprets catastrophe as chaos, the church interprets it as a summons to faith. To sing amid storm is to bear witness that Christ still reigns. Worship becomes both resistance to fear and allegiance to the throne. In every age, the faithful testify through song: "The kingdom of the world has become the kingdom of our Lord and of his Christ."

CONCLUSION

The trumpet visions remind us that history's turbulence is neither random nor final. Each blast echoes both warning and mercy—God's call for the world to awaken before judgment becomes irreversible. The silence in heaven, the rising prayers, and the restrained destruction all proclaim that divine justice is never out of control. Even evil must serve God's purposes until redemption is complete. For believers, the message is steadying: the same Lamb who opens the seals governs the storms. Our role is to pray, to worship, and to bear witness that repentance remains possible. The world may tremble, but the church stands firm, declaring through worship and endurance that the Lamb still reigns and will make all things new.

REFLECTION

1. Why do you think heaven falls silent before the trumpets begin to sound?

2. How do the prayers of the saints demonstrate faith in God's justice and sovereignty?

3. What does the repeated phrase "a third" reveal about the purpose of these judgments?

4. How does Revelation 8–9 challenge your view of evil's power in the world?

5. Where have you seen God use hardship or disruption to call people to repentance?

6. How does this passage shape the way you pray for a broken and rebellious world?

DISCUSSION

1. What does it mean for the church's worship and prayer to influence God's actions in history?

2. How can believers proclaim hope when the world interprets judgment only as despair?

3. Why is repentance so rare, even when people experience suffering or loss?

4. In what ways does Revelation show that evil operates under divine limits?

5. How can your congregation embody worship in a culture of fear and idolatry?

6. What would it look like to respond to global turmoil with confidence that the Lamb reigns?

8

THE LITTLE SCROLL & TWO WITNESSES

REVELATION 10–11

Objective: To call Christians to embrace their prophetic witness, enduring opposition while trusting Christ's ultimate victory.

INTRODUCTION

In 1989, a Chinese student stood alone in Tiananmen Square, blocking a line of military tanks. Armed with nothing but conviction, he refused to move. His courage became an image of defiance that echoed around the world. Though his fate remains uncertain, his stand still testifies that truth spoken in the face of power cannot be silenced forever.

That image captures the essence of Revelation 10–11. Between the sixth and seventh trumpets, John is called to receive and proclaim God's word, while the church is pictured as two witnesses standing against the powers of empire. They speak, suffer, and are seemingly silenced—but in the end, God vindicates them. Their story mirrors that of Christ himself.

These chapters remind believers that the church's mission is prophetic, not passive. We are called to "eat the book," to embody the gospel in a world that resists it. Our witness may be costly, but it is never wasted, for the Lamb will one day turn every act of faithful testimony into triumph.

EXAMINATION

The mighty angel and the open scroll (10:1-4)

Between the sixth and seventh trumpets, John witnesses an extraordinary vision. A mighty angel descends from heaven, wrapped in a cloud, with a rainbow over his head, his face shining like the sun, and his legs like pillars of fire. The description mirrors Christ's own appearance in Revelation 1, suggesting that this angel represents Christ's authority or acts as his messenger. The angel's stance—right foot on the sea and left on the land—symbolizes universal dominion. No part of creation lies outside divine authority.

The angel holds a "little scroll open in his hand." This scroll is the same one first seen in the right hand of God (5:1), but now unsealed and ready to be proclaimed. The fact that it is "little" may reflect its specific focus: the prophetic message John and the church are commissioned to deliver. When the angel roars like a lion, seven thunders respond with their own voices, but John is forbidden to write what they said. Revelation reminds us that even apocalyptic vision has limits—God reveals enough for faithfulness, not for curiosity. Some mysteries remain sealed until the end.

The oath and the finished mystery (10:5-7)

The angel lifts his right hand to heaven and swears by "him who lives forever and ever, who created heaven and what is in it, the earth and what is in it." The message is solemn: "There will be no more delay, but in the days of the trumpet call…the mystery of God would be fulfilled." This oath does not announce the immediate end of time but the certainty that God's plan for redemption and judgment is now moving toward completion.

The "mystery of God" is not something hidden but something once hidden and now revealed—the gospel itself (Rom. 16:25-26; Eph. 3:4-6). The Lamb's victory ensures that evil's apparent reign is temporary. John's readers, enduring persecution under Roman power, are reminded that history is not adrift. God's purposes may seem delayed, but they are neither forgotten nor frustrated. The same God who began creation will bring it to its appointed goal.

The scroll consumed and the prophet recommissioned (10:8-11)

A voice from heaven commands John to take the scroll and eat it. The image recalls Ezekiel 2-3, when the prophet ate a scroll filled with lamentation and woe. To "eat" the word means to internalize it—to let it shape one's heart, speech, and mission. John obeys: "It was sweet as honey in my mouth, but when I had eaten it my stomach was made bitter." God's message is always both sweet and bitter—sweet because it brings truth and redemption, bitter because it contains judgment and sorrow.

The voice then commissions him: "You must again prophesy about many peoples and nations and languages and kings." The prophetic call expands. John—and by extension, the church—is to bear witness to the world's powers. The people of God are not spectators of apocalypse but participants in it, proclaiming the gospel in a world that resists the Lamb. Revelation 10 thus shifts from vision to vocation. The prophet's task belongs to every disciple who bears the testimony of Jesus.

The measured temple and the trampled court (11:1-2)

John is given a measuring rod and told to measure the temple of God, the altar, and those who worship there. Like Ezekiel 40-48 and Zechariah 2, the act of measuring symbolizes divine protection and preservation. The temple here is not a literal structure but a symbol of the church—the dwelling place of God among his people. The measuring signifies that the inner reality of the church (true Christians) is secure, though the outer court (the visible church exposed to the world) will be trampled by the nations for forty-two months.

This "forty-two months" (or 1,260 days, or three and a half years) represents the entire period between Christ's ascension and return—a time of persecution and perseverance. The number, half of seven, portrays incompleteness: evil's power is limited. The church's security is spiritual, not physical. God does not promise exemption from suffering but endurance through it. Revelation thus balances comfort and challenge: the measured temple will stand, yet it will stand in a battlefield.

The two witnesses (11:3-6)

John now sees two witnesses clothed in sackcloth, prophesying for 1,260 days. The imagery is rich and layered. They are called "the two olive trees and the two lampstands," echoing Zechariah 4, where the olive trees supply oil to the lamps—symbols of the Spirit's empowering presence. The witnesses therefore represent the Spirit-filled church bearing testimony to Christ in a hostile world. Their "two-ness" reflects the Old Testament requirement for a valid testimony (Deut. 19:15); their message is legally and spiritually credible.

The description of their powers recalls Moses and Elijah—the ability to shut the sky (Elijah, 1 Kgs. 17:1) and turn water to blood or strike the earth with plagues (Moses, Exod. 7–12). These references signal continuity between the prophetic tradition and the church's mission. The people of God inherit the prophetic mantle. Their sackcloth signifies repentance and sorrow; their message exposes sin and calls for renewal. This is the essence of dissident discipleship: prophetic witness that confronts empire not with violence, but with truth spoken in love and endurance.

The witnesses slain and vindicated (11:7–13)

When they have finished their testimony, "the beast that rises from the bottomless pit" makes war on them and kills them. This is the first mention of the beast, later described in chapter 13. Here it represents the political and cultural powers of the world that oppose God's truth. The bodies of the witnesses lie in the street of the "great city," symbolically called Sodom and Egypt—terms evoking moral corruption and spiritual oppression. John adds, "where their Lord was crucified," identifying the city with any place where Christ is rejected.

The sight of their corpses becomes a grotesque celebration. "Those who dwell on the earth rejoice…because these two prophets had been a torment to them." This is the world's response to faithful witness—mockery and temporary triumph. Yet after three and a half days, "a breath of life from God entered them." They stand on their feet, and great fear falls on those who see them. Their ascension in a cloud recalls both Elijah and Christ, symbolizing vindication and resurrection. The earthquake that follows kills some and terrifies others into giving glory to God.

The pattern is unmistakable: the church's mission mirrors the Lamb's. Testimony leads to suffering, suffering to apparent defeat, and defeat to ultimate victory. The world may silence the witnesses, but it cannot cancel their resurrection. This is not prediction of individual events but description of a recurring reality—the rhythm of Christian witness in every generation.

The seventh trumpet: Heaven's declaration of victory (11:15–19)

At last the seventh angel sounds his trumpet, and loud voices in heaven proclaim, "The kingdom of the world has become the kingdom of our Lord and of his Christ, and he shall reign forever and ever." The waiting ends, the mystery of God is complete, and the voices of the twenty-four elders respond with worship. They give thanks that God's reign has come in its fullness—that the time has arrived for judging the dead, rewarding the faithful, and destroying those who destroy the earth.

The vision ends where it began—with the temple in heaven opened and the ark of the covenant visible. Lightning, thunder, and earthquake once more signal God's presence. The hidden covenant is now revealed; the promise made to Abraham and fulfilled in Christ has reached its goal. What was partial becomes permanent; what was threatened becomes secure. The kingdom that began in weakness is consummated in glory.

Witness and worship in a hostile world

Revelation 10–11 teaches that God's people are not spectators but participants in his redemptive plan. The open scroll calls the church to receive God's word inwardly and proclaim it publicly. The measured temple reassures believers that, though pressed and persecuted, they are secure in God's care. The two witnesses reveal the church's mission: to bear truthful testimony in the face of opposition, trusting that vindication belongs to God. The seventh trumpet confirms that all of history moves toward worship, not despair.

The church resists empire not by violence but by faithfulness—by embodying the Lamb's pattern of witness, suffering, and triumph. The little scroll commissions every Christian to speak the truth of the gospel even when the world prefers silence. The two witnesses remind us that the church's apparent defeat often precedes its most powerful testimony. And the seventh trumpet assures us that the outcome is certain: the kingdoms of this world will become the kingdom of Christ.

The church's calling, then, is both prophetic and hopeful—to eat the scroll, proclaim the word, endure persecution, and trust that the final sound we hear will not be the trumpet of terror, but the anthem of victory.

APPLICATION

1. God's word must be consumed before it can be proclaimed

When John was told to eat the scroll, he discovered that God's message was both sweet and bitter. That remains true for every believer. Scripture nourishes the soul, but it also convicts the heart. The church cannot speak for God until it has first listened to him deeply. To "eat the book" is to internalize the gospel—to let it shape our thoughts, words, and compassion. We cannot proclaim comfort without also announcing judgment; we cannot offer grace without confronting sin. Effective witness begins with digestion, not declaration. God calls his church to absorb the word until it transforms us, and then to speak that truth, no matter how costly or unpopular it may be.

2. Faithful witness will bring opposition but also vindication

The story of the two witnesses mirrors the life of Jesus—ministry, suffering, death, and resurrection. Their experience teaches the church that faithful witness will provoke hostility. The world celebrates when truth seems silenced, but God always has the last word. Resurrection follows rejection; vindication follows suffering. Believers should not measure success by safety or popularity, but by faithfulness to their calling. Even when the church appears defeated, its testimony endures. Every act of courage, every word of truth spoken in love, participates in Christ's triumph. The power of witness lies not in persuasion but in perseverance. The God who raised the witnesses will raise his people too, proving that the message of the Lamb cannot be buried.

3. The church is secure though not spared from suffering

John's vision of the measured temple offers a tension every Christian must hold: the church is protected spiritually even as it suffers physically. God's measurement assures that his people belong to him and cannot be lost, yet the outer court is trampled. This means the church's security is not exemption from pain but preservation through it. Christians can face persecution, cultural hostility, or loss with confidence that God has already marked them as his own. The enemy may bruise the body, but he cannot touch the soul.

The measuring rod in John's hand becomes the promise in ours: our lives are defined by God's boundary, not the world's threat. To live as the measured people of God is to endure suffering without surrendering hope.

4. The church's mission is to bear witness

The seventh trumpet announces the final reality: "The kingdom of the world has become the kingdom of our Lord and of his Christ." That outcome is certain, but the church's task continues until that day. Revelation 10-11 reminds us that history's midpoint belongs to proclamation. The little scroll commissions the church to speak; the witnesses embody that call through word and deed. Our mission is not to conquer culture but to testify faithfully to the Lamb's reign. In a world chasing comfort, witness demands courage. In an age drowning in noise, witness requires clarity. Every sermon, conversation, and act of love declares that Christ already reigns. The church does not bring the kingdom through force but reflects it through faithfulness—trusting that the trumpet's final sound will vindicate every word spoken for his glory.

CONCLUSION

Revelation 10-11 calls the church to a mission both sobering and glorious. We are a people who have eaten the scroll—shaped by God's word, sweet with grace and bitter with truth. Our task is to testify in a world that often mocks or resists that message, knowing that faithfulness may lead to suffering. Yet the two witnesses remind us that apparent defeat never has the final word. The God who raised them will also vindicate his people. When the seventh trumpet sounds, every act of courage, every whispered prayer, and every word of truth will resound in heaven's victory song: "The kingdom of the world has become the kingdom of our Lord and of his Christ."

REFLECTION

1. What does the sweetness and bitterness of the little scroll teach about speaking God's truth?

2. How does the image of the measured temple comfort believers facing hardship or persecution?

3. Why do you think God's message is often resisted or silenced by the world?

4. In what ways does the story of the two witnesses mirror Jesus' own ministry and resurrection?

5. How does the seventh trumpet assure Christians that their endurance is not in vain?

6. What would change in your walk with Christ if you viewed your life as a prophetic witness?

DISCUSSION

1. What does it mean to "eat the book" before proclaiming God's word in today's world?

2. How can the church remain faithful when truth-telling leads to rejection or ridicule?

3. Why is it important that the church's security is spiritual rather than political or physical?

4. What practical forms of witness demonstrate the church's allegiance to the Lamb?

5. How does Revelation 11 challenge our definition of victory and success in ministry?

6. What encouragement do you draw from knowing that the kingdom already belongs to Christ?

9

THE DRAGON & THE BEASTS
REVELATION 12–14

Objective: To equip Christians to discern deception and remain faithful amid worldly power and spiritual opposition.

INTRODUCTION

In 1937, German pastor Martin Niemöller was arrested for refusing to pledge allegiance to Adolf Hitler. From his prison cell he later wrote, "It took me a long time to learn that God's kingdom does not come through the strength of nations, but through the weakness of the cross." His courage became a symbol of resistance to tyranny and of loyalty to a higher throne.

That same tension runs through Revelation 12–13. John pulls back the curtain to show the powers behind persecution—the dragon who wages war against the saints, and the two beasts who deceive the world into worshiping false power. The first beast dominates through political might; the second seduces through religious and cultural persuasion. Together, they mimic God's authority to claim human allegiance.

Yet amid the rage of the dragon stands the Lamb's people—those sealed by God, who overcome by faith and perseverance. Revelation invites believers not to panic or compromise, but to see through deception and hold fast to the truth: evil imitates, but it cannot conquer. The Lamb has already triumphed, and his followers bear witness to that victory by their enduring faithfulness.

EXAMINATION

The woman, the child, and the dragon (12:1-6)

John's vision begins not with beasts or battles but with a woman clothed with the sun, the moon under her feet, and a crown of twelve stars. This radiant figure symbolizes the people of God in their fullness—first Israel, then the church, the covenant community through whom God brings forth the Messiah. She is pregnant and cries out in labor, ready to give birth. The child she bears is the promised ruler, the one destined "to rule all the nations with a rod of iron" (Ps. 2:9).

Opposite her stands a great red dragon with seven heads and ten horns, symbols of immense power and cruelty. The dragon is explicitly identified as "that ancient serpent, who is called the devil and Satan." His tail sweeps a third of the stars from heaven, showing his destructive influence over fallen angels. As the woman gives birth, the dragon crouches, ready to devour her child. But his plan fails. The child is caught up to God and to his throne—a single phrase summarizing Christ's incarnation, victory, and ascension.

The woman flees into the wilderness, where God nourishes her for 1,260 days. The wilderness symbolizes divine protection amid danger, echoing Israel's journey through the desert and Elijah's refuge by the brook. The wilderness is not comfort but safety—God's hidden place for his people between Christ's ascension and return.

War in heaven and Satan's defeat (12:7-12)

The scene shifts from earth to heaven, where Michael and his angels wage war against the dragon. This battle is not a literal celestial sword fight but a symbolic depiction of Satan's defeat through Christ's death and resurrection. The "casting down" of the accuser signifies that the devil no longer has power to condemn the saints before God's throne. His accusations are silenced by the blood of the Lamb.

A loud voice in heaven declares victory: "Now the salvation and the power and the kingdom of our God and the authority of his Christ have come." The faithful conquer "by the blood of the Lamb and by the word of their testimony, for they loved not their lives even unto death." This is the theology of Revelation in miniature—Christ's victory empowers the church's witness. The dragon is furious because his time is short. Defeated in heaven, he now rages on earth, targeting those who belong to the Lamb. The church is not spared from Satan's wrath but sustained in the midst of it. The cosmic victory of Christ becomes the daily endurance of Christians.

The dragon's war against the woman's offspring (12:13–17)

Cast down to earth, the dragon pursues the woman, but she is given "two wings of the great eagle" to fly to her wilderness refuge. This recalls God's protection of Israel: "I bore you on eagles' wings and brought you to myself" (Exod. 19:4). The serpent spews a river to sweep her away, a torrent of persecution and deception, but the earth swallows the flood, symbolizing divine intervention.

Frustrated, the dragon turns his fury toward "the rest of her offspring," those "who keep the commandments of God and hold to the testimony of Jesus." This phrase defines the church's identity and mission. Believers are both obedient and witness-bearing. The dragon's rage against them is proof of their faithfulness. Revelation 12 exposes the unseen dimension of persecution: behind every emperor, ideology, or false religion stands the same adversary. Yet even his fury is futile. The Lamb's people may be harassed, but they are not overcome.

The beast from the sea (13:1–10)

Standing on the shore, the dragon summons a beast from the sea—an image that would have stirred fear in ancient minds. The sea represented chaos, danger, and untamed evil. This beast has ten horns and seven heads, like the dragon, showing that it is his earthly proxy. It blends features of Daniel's four beasts (Dan. 7), representing a composite of empires—Babylon, Persia, Greece, and Rome. It is political power animated by satanic ambition.

The beast receives the dragon's throne and authority. One of its heads appears mortally wounded but healed, a parody of Christ's death and resurrection. This imitation is the essence of evil—it mimics the divine while denying its holiness. The world marvels and worships the beast, asking, "Who is like the beast, and who can fight against it?" This is blasphemous parody of the worship of God: "Who is like the Lord?" (Exod. 15:11). The beast is given power for forty-two months, the symbolic period of persecution throughout the church age.

This beast speaks proud words, wages war on the saints, and conquers them—outwardly, not spiritually. Believers may be killed, but their faith remains victorious. Verse 10 issues the defining call: "Here is a call for the endurance and faith of the saints." Political power that demands worship is the beast in every age. In John's world, it was Rome; in ours, it can be any system that exalts itself against God. Revelation unmasks the idolatry of empire and summons the church to steadfast loyalty to the Lamb.

The beast from the earth (13:11–17)

A second beast rises from the earth, completing the unholy trinity. This beast has two horns like a lamb but speaks like a dragon—a counterfeit Christ who uses religious appearance for demonic ends. Later called "the false prophet" (16:13; 19:20), he represents all spiritual, cultural, or ideological systems that persuade people to worship the first beast.

The land-beast performs great signs, even calling fire from heaven, echoing Elijah's miracles and the Spirit's descent at Pentecost. His counterfeit wonders deceive those who dwell on the earth. He constructs an image of the first beast and gives it breath, mimicking the Spirit who breathes life into believers. Through deception, he convinces humanity to worship power itself.

This second beast represents propaganda—whether religious, political, or cultural—that sanctifies empire and turns citizens into worshipers of the state. In John's day, that took the form of emperor worship enforced by local cults. Today it may appear as nationalism, consumerism, or ideology that replaces God with human authority. The beast persuades people to receive a "mark" on their right hand or forehead—symbols of thought and action. Just as believers are sealed by God (7:3), the beast's followers are marked by their allegiance to worldly power.

The number of the beast (13:18)

John concludes with a riddle: "Let the one who has understanding calculate the number of the beast, for it is the number of a man, and his number is 666." Throughout history, interpreters have speculated about its identity. The number likely refers symbolically to Nero Caesar when written in Hebrew letters, but its meaning transcends any single person. Six falls short of seven—the number of perfection—three times over. Evil is repetition without fulfillment, parody without completion. The beast's number stands for humanity in perpetual rebellion—power that imitates God but never equals him.

Every empire, every ideology that demands worship, bears the mark of 666. The church's task is discernment—to recognize the beastly patterns of our own age and refuse compromise. The mark is not a barcode or implant but a spiritual orientation: what we think, what we value, what we serve. Revelation asks not who the beast *is* but whose mark *we* bear.

The call to endurance and discernment

Revelation 12–13 portrays the cosmic war behind the church's struggle on earth. Satan's defeat at the cross is final, but his opposition is fierce. He cannot touch the throne, so he attacks the church. His two beasts—political coercion and spiritual deception—still work to win human allegiance. Yet believers need not fear. The same voice that cast down the accuser also declares the saints victorious.

These chapters equip the church for resistance, not retreat. The faithful overcome by worship, truth, and endurance. Evil's greatest weapon is imitation, but discernment exposes its counterfeit nature. Every generation must learn to recognize the beasts of its time and to confess with courage that the Lamb alone is worthy. The wilderness may be harsh, but it is holy ground where God preserves his people.

For John's readers, Rome was the beast that demanded worship and punished dissent. For later generations, the beast has worn other masks—totalitarianism, nationalism, greed, or ideology. Yet the message remains: no earthly power deserves the loyalty that belongs to the Lamb. The believer's endurance is not passive suffering but active allegiance.

The victory behind the conflict

Revelation 12–13 lifts the veil on spiritual reality. The dragon rages because he has already lost. The beasts deceive because they cannot create. The church suffers but cannot be destroyed. Every page echoes the same truth: Christ reigns, and his people conquer by faithfulness, not force.

The cry of heaven in chapter 12—"They conquered him by the blood of the Lamb"—defines Christian identity. The cross was the true battlefield; the resurrection was the decisive victory. The church's task is to live out that triumph in patient endurance. As the dragon prowls and the beasts blaspheme, the faithful hold fast, marked not by fear but by faith.

Revelation 13 ends with human arrogance—666—but chapter 14 will begin with divine completeness—144,000 standing with the Lamb.

Between those two visions lies the church's vocation: to endure, to discern, and to bear witness that the Lamb's name is greater than any empire's mark.

APPLICATION

1. Christ's victory defines our reality, not Satan's rage

Revelation 12 unveils the unseen world behind the church's suffering. The dragon rages not because he is strong, but because he is defeated. His fury is the desperation of a fallen enemy. Christians often feel overwhelmed by evil's persistence, yet this vision reminds us that the decisive battle has already been won at the cross. The accuser has been thrown down, and his accusations silenced by the Lamb's blood. We do not fight for victory but from it. When chaos shakes our world, we stand firm in the assurance that Christ's triumph is permanent. Satan may roar, but he cannot reclaim what grace has secured. Every act of faithfulness—every prayer, every refusal to compromise—is a declaration that the dragon's time is short and the Lamb's reign is forever.

2. The beasts expose worldly power and false religion

The two beasts show how evil disguises itself. The first beast embodies political and cultural systems that demand loyalty and worship. The second beast, appearing gentle as a lamb, uses ideology, religion, and persuasion to sanctify that power. Together they mimic the Father and Son, forming an unholy trinity that imitates but cannot recreate God's authority. Revelation unmasks their deception. It warns the church that the greatest threats are not external violence but subtle compromise—when Christians trade allegiance to the Lamb for allegiance to worldly success or security. Discernment requires recognizing when the state, the market, or even religion itself begins to speak like a dragon. To resist the beasts is to remain loyal to Christ alone, refusing to let any earthly power define what only God can command.

3. Endurance and discernment are acts of worship

Twice in these chapters John calls for "endurance and faith." Perseverance is not passive waiting but active worship. To endure is to keep singing the Lamb's song in the midst of the dragon's noise. Discernment guards that endurance; it teaches believers to see beyond appearances. Evil often arrives dressed as good—success, patriotism, or comfort—but its voice always demands compromise. The faithful must learn to test every spirit and to measure every loyalty against the cross. Endurance is the courage to suffer rather than surrender, to witness rather than conform. It is how the church worships under pressure. When Christians live with patience and clarity, they announce that Christ's kingdom has already come and that the world's powers are only temporary imitations of his rule.

4. Allegiance to the Lamb marks the faithful

The mark of the beast is not a future technology but a present choice—allegiance expressed in thought and action. To receive God's seal or the beast's mark is to reveal one's true loyalty. Revelation 13 forces believers to ask hard questions: Whose approval do I seek? Whose authority shapes my ethics, my politics, my worship? Those sealed by God bear his name on their foreheads, living with minds and hands devoted to his will. The beast's mark belongs to those who define success and security apart from Christ. In every generation, the church faces that choice of allegiance. The world calls for compromise; the Lamb calls for faithfulness. To be marked by the Lamb is to bear witness that even in a world ruled by imitation thrones, Jesus alone is Lord.

CONCLUSION

Revelation 12–13 reminds believers that the world's struggles are not merely political or cultural—they are spiritual. Behind every empire's pride and every false religion's charm stands the same dragon, enraged but defeated. His beasts still demand allegiance, but their power is temporary and their imitation hollow. The faithful overcome not by strength but by steadfast loyalty to the Lamb. Endurance, worship, and discernment remain the church's greatest weapons. Though the conflict rages, the outcome is certain: the accuser has been cast down, and the kingdom already belongs to Christ. In every age, the church's task is the same—to refuse the mark of fear and to bear the name of the Lamb in courageous faithfulness.

REFLECTION

1. How does the vision of the dragon deepen your understanding of spiritual warfare?
2. What comfort do you find in knowing that Satan's rage flows from his defeat?
3. In what ways do the two beasts imitate God's power and seek human allegiance?
4. How can Christians discern when political or religious systems become idolatrous?
5. What does it mean to be sealed by God in a world marked by compromise?
6. How does Revelation 12–13 strengthen your resolve to remain faithful to Christ?

DISCUSSION

1. How does Revelation's portrait of the dragon and beasts explain the church's struggles today?
2. What modern examples reflect the deceptive power of the second beast's propaganda?
3. Why is endurance such an essential part of worship and discipleship in Revelation?
4. How might Christians resist subtle pressures to conform to worldly values or power?
5. What practical steps help a congregation live out allegiance to the Lamb above all else?
6. How does this passage call believers to courage, hope, and discernment in a hostile world?

10

THE HARVEST & THE BOWLS

REVELATION 14–16

Objective: To strengthen Christians' hope by showing God's justice as the completion of his redeeming love.

INTRODUCTION

In 1863, President Abraham Lincoln stood on the battlefield of Gettysburg and said that the nation must ensure "these dead shall not have died in vain." His words acknowledged both the tragedy and the necessity of justice—the cost of restoring what evil had torn apart. History's turning points often come with grief and glory intertwined.

Revelation 14–16 captures a similar tension on a cosmic scale. Heaven sings even as judgment falls. The redeemed stand secure with the Lamb on Mount Zion while the bowls of wrath are poured out on a world that refused repentance. These chapters reveal that God's justice is neither arbitrary nor cruel—it is the completion of redemption. Evil must be judged for creation to be healed.

For the church, this vision is not meant to frighten but to steady. The final harvest reminds believers that their endurance is not in vain and that God's judgments, though severe, are right and true. When the voice from heaven declares, "It is done," the faithful can rest knowing that every wrong will be made right and every tear will give way to triumph.

EXAMINATION

The Lamb and the redeemed on Mount Zion (14:1–5)

After the terrifying visions of the dragon and the beasts, John's eyes are lifted to a scene of triumph. "Then I looked, and behold, on Mount Zion stood the Lamb, and with him 144,000 who had his name and his Father's name written on their foreheads." Evil may rage on earth, but the first image of chapter 14 reminds believers that the Lamb still reigns and his people stand secure. The number 144,000, as in chapter 7, symbolizes the totality of God's redeemed—complete, preserved, and loyal.

They stand with the Lamb, not cowering before the beast. Their song is the "new song" of redemption—known only to those purchased by Christ's blood. Their purity is spiritual faithfulness, described in imagery of chastity: they have not defiled themselves with spiritual adultery, and they follow the Lamb wherever he goes. They are called "firstfruits," anticipating the final harvest of the redeemed. This vision anchors the church's hope: those marked by the Lamb's name will never be erased by the beast's mark.

The three angelic messages (14:6–13)

The focus shifts from Zion to heaven's messengers, each carrying a proclamation that interprets history from God's perspective.

The first angel proclaims "an eternal gospel" to every nation, tribe, language, and people, saying, "Fear God and give him glory, because the hour of his judgment has come." In Revelation, the gospel is not sentimental optimism but the call to repentance and allegiance to the Creator. The summons to worship God "who made heaven and earth" counters the imperial idolatry that demanded worship of Rome's rulers.

The second angel announces Babylon's fall—an event not yet narrated but certain in God's plan. "Fallen, fallen is Babylon the great, she who made all nations drink the wine of the passion of her sexual immorality." Babylon personifies the world's seductive power—wealth, pleasure, and pride that intoxicate nations and defile souls. Though Babylon still seems to prosper, her doom is inevitable.

The third angel warns against worshiping the beast or receiving its mark. The imagery of torment "in fire and sulfur" expresses not sadism but solemn justice—the eternal consequence of idolatry. The call that follows in verse 12 summarizes the entire vision: "Here is a call for the endurance of the saints, those who keep the commandments of God and their faith in Jesus." Faithfulness in suffering is the fruit of trust in God's sovereignty. Then comes a voice from heaven declaring blessing on those who die in the Lord: "They may rest from their labors, for their deeds follow them."

These three proclamations confront the church with a stark choice—Babylon or Zion, the beast's mark or the Lamb's name, temporary comfort or eternal rest.

The harvest of the earth (14:14–20)

John next sees "a white cloud, and seated on the cloud one like a son of man." The imagery recalls Daniel 7:13 and Jesus' own words about the final judgment (Matt. 13:39–43). The one on the cloud, crowned with gold and holding a sharp sickle, represents Christ himself, harvesting the earth. An angel calls for the reaping of the grain—the harvest of the righteous, symbolizing salvation. Another angel, with authority over fire, commands a second harvest—the gathering of grapes into the winepress of God's wrath.

The two harvests together depict the final separation of humanity: salvation and judgment. The winepress imagery echoes Isaiah 63:3, where God tramples the nations in judgment. Blood flows "as high as a horse's bridle for 1,600 stadia"—a number suggesting completeness ($4 \times 4 \times 10 \times 10$). The point is not geography but gravity: God's justice is thorough and inescapable.

The harvest assures believers that evil will not go unanswered. The Lamb who redeems will also judge. For the faithful, judgment is not terror but vindication—the moment when righteousness is revealed and creation is restored.

The song of Moses and the Lamb (15:1–4)

After judgment imagery comes worship once again. John sees another sign in heaven: seven angels with seven plagues, "which are the last, for with them the wrath of God is finished." Before the bowls are poured out, heaven pauses to sing. The redeemed stand beside a "sea of glass mingled with fire," representing both peace and purity in God's presence.

They sing "the song of Moses, the servant of God, and the song of the Lamb," uniting the exodus and the cross. The two songs tell one story—deliverance through divine victory. The lyrics proclaim God's justice and glory:

"Great and amazing are your deeds, O Lord God the Almighty! ... All nations will come and worship you." The judgments to come are therefore not contradictions of God's goodness but expressions of it. He is praised not only for mercy but for justice that restores creation and vindicates the oppressed.

Worship frames Revelation's vision of wrath. Before the bowls are poured, believers are reminded that judgment flows from holiness, not cruelty. The song of Moses and the Lamb calls the church to worship God for his righteous acts, even when they unsettle the world.

The sanctuary opened and the bowls given (15:5-8)

John sees the heavenly temple—the tabernacle of testimony—opened. Seven angels emerge, clothed in pure linen and golden sashes, ready to carry out God's decrees. One of the four living creatures gives them seven golden bowls filled with the wrath of God. As they depart, "the temple was filled with smoke from the glory of God and from his power." The image recalls the dedication of the tabernacle (Exod. 40:34-35) and the temple (1 Kgs. 8:10-11), when God's presence filled the sanctuary so completely that none could enter.

Here, the fullness of divine glory means the time for intercession is over. The bowls signify that judgment is not arbitrary; it arises from the holy character of God. What began with the prayers of the saints (8:3-5) now concludes with God's answer. Justice delayed is not justice denied—it is justice fulfilled at the proper time.

The first five bowls: Justice and hardness (16:1-11)

The angels pour out their bowls, unleashing judgments that echo the plagues of Egypt. Painful sores afflict those who bear the beast's mark. The sea and rivers turn to blood, showing that creation itself testifies against idolatry. The sun scorches humanity with fierce heat, yet instead of repenting, people curse God. Darkness descends on the beast's kingdom, exposing its impotence.

The angel of the waters declares the righteousness of God's acts: "You are just, O Holy One, because you have brought these judgments." The world's refusal to repent reveals sin's true depth. Even in the face of undeniable truth, rebellion persists. The repeated refrain—"they did not repent"—underscores that judgment hardens those who have already rejected grace. The faithful are reminded that their suffering is temporary, but sin's defiance is eternal unless surrendered to the Lamb.

The sixth bowl: The gathering at Armageddon (16:12–16)

The sixth bowl dries up the Euphrates River, preparing the way for the kings of the east. This allusion recalls how God dried the Red Sea for Israel's deliverance, but now the path is cleared for destruction. Three unclean spirits—like frogs—emerge from the mouths of the dragon, the beast, and the false prophet. They perform miraculous signs, deceiving the nations to assemble for "the great day of God the Almighty."

The name "Armageddon," from the Hebrew *Har-Megiddo* (Mount Megiddo), is symbolic. Megiddo was a historic battlefield in Israel, a place of decisive conflict. Yet no literal mountain fits this name; it represents the final confrontation between good and evil. Revelation presents Armageddon not as a geographic location but as a theological reality: the culmination of humanity's rebellion against God, destined to fail.

In the midst of this dark vision, Christ interjects: "Behold, I am coming like a thief! Blessed is the one who stays awake, keeping his garments on." Even at the height of judgment, Christians are called to vigilance and purity. Armageddon is not an event to fear but a reminder that Christ's coming will surprise the unprepared and vindicate the faithful.

The seventh bowl: "It is done" (16:17–21)

The final bowl is poured into the air, symbolizing the completion of divine wrath over all creation. A loud voice from the throne declares, "It is done!"—echoing Christ's cry from the cross, "It is finished." What began in redemption now concludes in judgment. Lightning, thunder, and an unprecedented earthquake shake the world. Babylon the great splits apart, and the cities of the nations fall. Giant hailstones descend, recalling the plagues of Egypt and prefiguring final judgment.

Yet even now, "they cursed God for the plague of the hail." The impenitence of the wicked contrasts sharply with the worship of the redeemed. The same justice that comforts the saints condemns the unrepentant. For the faithful, "It is done" signals not dread but deliverance. God's wrath is not the loss of control but the completion of righteousness. The story of Revelation moves toward restoration, not ruin.

The God who judges and redeems

Revelation 14-16 completes the cycle of visions begun with the seals and trumpets. Each series portrays the same divine sovereignty from a different angle: the seals reveal history's endurance, the trumpets warn the unrepentant, and the bowls execute final justice. Through it all, the central truth stands—the Lord reigns.

God's kingdom confronts every empire, calling the faithful to worship and the wicked to repentance. Judgment is not divine temper but divine truth, the necessary conclusion of a holy love that refuses to ignore evil. The Lamb who bears the world's sin also bears the world's authority. For the church, these visions are not blueprints for prediction but assurances for perseverance.

The saints sing, the angels pour, and heaven declares, "It is done." Between the Lamb's cross and his coming, the church continues to bear witness—trusting that justice will be complete, mercy vindicated, and every song of faith joined in the final chorus of the redeemed.

APPLICATION

1. The Lamb's triumph anchors the church's endurance

The vision of the 144,000 standing with the Lamb reminds believers that their security does not rest on circumstances but on covenant. They bear his name, not the beast's mark. In every age, the faithful endure because their identity is settled in Christ's victory. When the powers of the world threaten or entice, the people of God remember that their place is already with the Lamb on Mount Zion. This vision calls the church to confidence, not complacency. Endurance flows from assurance: because the Lamb reigns, we can stand. Every act of perseverance, every refusal to compromise, becomes a testimony that the kingdom of God is unshakable. The world's systems collapse, but the Lamb's people remain, singing the new song of redemption.

2. God's justice is holy, complete, and worthy of worship

Revelation's judgments unsettle modern readers, yet they reveal God's righteousness, not cruelty. The bowls of wrath flow from the same throne that once sent the Son to the cross. The angel's words—"You are just, O Holy One"—remind us that divine anger is never arbitrary. It is the holy response of love to evil that refuses repentance. For the oppressed, judgment is not vengeance but vindication; for the faithful, it is not fear but fulfillment. The song of Moses and the Lamb teaches Christians to praise God even for justice that purges creation of corruption. True worship acknowledges both mercy and wrath. The redeemed celebrate God's judgments because they reveal his character—perfect holiness that refuses to coexist with sin and will one day make all things right.

3. The world's rebellion exposes the hardness of unbelief

Twice in Revelation 16 we read that humanity "did not repent." Even when faced with undeniable evidence of divine power, the world curses God rather than seeks him. This shows that sin is not ignorance but obstinacy. The human heart, apart from grace, resists the very mercy that could save it. The church must read these passages not with pride but with humility, remembering that repentance is a gift of God's Spirit. Our task is to bear witness with urgency, proclaiming both warning and hope. Every refusal to repent deepens rebellion; every humble confession opens the way to life. Revelation warns Christians not to confuse patience with apathy—God's delay is mercy, not neglect. The church must use this time to call the world from hardness to holiness.

4. Worship prepares believers for final victory

Before judgment falls, heaven sings. That order is intentional. Worship centers the church in truth before the chaos of the world unfolds. The saints by the sea of glass lift their voices not in panic but in praise, declaring that God's ways are righteous. Their example teaches us that worship is not a retreat from reality but the strength to face it. When we worship, we proclaim that God's rule is good even when his justice is severe. Every Sunday gathering, every hymn, every prayer rehearses the victory of the Lamb and prepares the church for endurance. Worship is resistance. It refuses fear and reminds the faithful that the story ends not with wrath alone but with redemption fulfilled and a chorus that sings, "Great and amazing are your deeds, O Lord God Almighty."

CONCLUSION

Revelation 14–16 brings the story of divine justice to its climax. The redeemed stand with the Lamb, the angels proclaim judgment and mercy, and the bowls of wrath reveal God's holiness in full. Evil's collapse and Babylon's fall are not the end of hope but the dawn of restoration. The voice that once said on the cross, "It is finished," now declares from heaven, "It is done." For believers, that declaration means victory secured and redemption complete. The world's rebellion will not have the last word—the Lamb will. Until that day, the church endures in worship, proclaiming that the God who judges is also the God who saves, and his kingdom will never end.

REFLECTION

1. What encouragement does the image of the 144,000 with the Lamb offer you personally?

2. How does Revelation 14 remind believers that worship and endurance belong together?

3. Why is it important to view God's justice as an expression of his holiness and love?

4. What do the repeated refusals to repent in chapter 16 reveal about the human heart?

5. How does the song of Moses and the Lamb deepen your understanding of worship?

6. What assurance do you find in hearing heaven's voice declare, "It is done"?

DISCUSSION

1. How can the church stand firm in faith when surrounded by the world's corruption?

2. In what ways should Christians celebrate God's justice without becoming vengeful?

3. What lessons does Revelation 16 teach about the danger of hardening the heart?

4. How can worship serve as both comfort and resistance for believers today?

5. Why does Revelation pair songs of praise with scenes of judgment?

6. How might the certainty of the Lamb's triumph change how we live, work, and witness now?

11

THE FALL OF BABYLON
REVELATION 17-18

Objective: To warn Christians against Babylon's seduction and strengthen confidence in the Lamb's enduring kingdom.

INTRODUCTION

In AD 79, the wealthy city of Pompeii thrived in the shadow of Mount Vesuvius. Its streets bustled with trade, art, and entertainment. Then, without warning, the volcano erupted, burying the city in ash. Centuries later, archaeologists uncovered frescoes, temples, and homes frozen in time—monuments to a society that believed its pleasures would never end.

That story echoes in Revelation 17-18. John describes another great city—Babylon—radiant with splendor, powerful in politics, and unmatched in wealth. Yet her beauty masks her corruption. She has intoxicated the nations with luxury and immorality, persecuted the saints, and glorified herself instead of God. Her downfall comes suddenly, decisively, and completely. The empires of the world may glitter like gold, but their foundations are sand.

For believers, this vision is both warning and comfort. Babylon's collapse reveals that no power, no economy, and no culture that defies God can endure. But for those who follow the Lamb, her ruin means release. The kingdoms of the world fall, but the kingdom of Christ stands forever.

EXAMINATION

The woman and the beast (17:1-6)

One of the angels who poured out the bowls invites John to witness the judgment of "the great prostitute who is seated on many waters." The image of a prostitute captures the nature of Babylon's influence—she seduces, entices, and corrupts. She represents not a single city but the spiritual character of every culture that abandons God for power, wealth, and pleasure. The "many waters" symbolize the nations over which her influence spreads. She intoxicates the kings of the earth with her immorality and entices the world to join her in rebellion.

John sees her sitting on a scarlet beast, full of blasphemous names and adorned with seven heads and ten horns. The beast is the same empire-beast of chapter 13, now ridden by a woman clothed in purple and scarlet, glittering with gold and jewels. Her outward splendor hides inward corruption. She holds a golden cup, but it is filled with abominations. Written on her forehead are the words, "Babylon the great, mother of prostitutes and of earth's abominations." She is drunk with the blood of the saints—a vivid picture of worldly systems that enrich themselves by oppressing the faithful.

For John's readers, this woman clearly symbolized Rome—the city that ruled the world with seductive luxury and cruel persecution. Yet Babylon's face changes across generations. She represents any civilization that replaces worship with self-indulgence, morality with marketing, and holiness with prosperity. Every empire that enthrones power and pleasure above God carries her name.

The mystery explained (17:7-14)

The angel explains the mystery of the woman and the beast. The beast "was, and is not, and is about to rise from the bottomless pit." The language mimics the divine title of God, "who was, and is, and is to come." Evil always imitates but never equals God. The beast's temporary revival parodies resurrection—political power that seems to die and return in new forms. Humanity marvels, but heaven sees the truth: its destruction is inevitable.

The seven heads represent seven hills—an unmistakable reference to Rome—but they also symbolize a succession of kingdoms. The ten horns stand for kings or powers that will align briefly with the beast before turning against Babylon. Their reign is limited—"for one hour"—a reminder that every empire's power is temporary. The world's coalitions rise and fall, but their story always ends the same way: "They will make war on the Lamb, and the Lamb will conquer them, for he is Lord of lords and King of kings."

This declaration stands at the center of the vision. Evil is powerful, organized, and alluring, but it is not ultimate. The victory of the Lamb is not future speculation—it is present reality. His followers are called "chosen and faithful," standing firm amid the chaos. The saints conquer not by violence but by allegiance, resisting Babylon's seduction through obedience to Christ.

The beast turns on the woman (17:15–18)

The angel continues, explaining that the waters where the prostitute sits are "peoples and multitudes and nations and languages." Babylon's influence is universal; her corruption spreads through culture, economy, and ideology. Yet in a striking twist, the beast and its allies turn against her, stripping her bare and devouring her flesh. Evil consumes itself. The same political and economic forces that supported Babylon will destroy her when their interests shift.

John's readers would have recognized this dynamic in Rome's fragile alliances and moral decay. But the principle applies across history: every godless empire eventually collapses under its own corruption. What the world worships as stability is an illusion. The angel concludes, "God has put it into their hearts to carry out his purpose." Even their rebellion serves divine sovereignty. God's justice does not merely oppose evil—it uses evil to undo itself. The chapter ends by identifying the woman as "the great city that has dominion over the kings of the earth." Babylon is the city that never learns, the system that always returns, until the final judgment brings her down forever.

Babylon's fall announced (18:1–8)

John sees another angel descending from heaven, shining with divine glory and proclaiming, "Fallen, fallen is Babylon the great!" The repetition underscores certainty. What John sees as future is already accomplished in God's plan. Babylon's downfall is inevitable because her sins have "heaped up as high as heaven." She has glorified herself, lived in luxury, and claimed,

"I sit as queen, I am no widow, and mourning I shall never see." Her pride mirrors ancient Babylon's arrogance and Rome's self-deification.

Then comes a call to the faithful: "Come out of her, my people, lest you take part in her sins, lest you share in her plagues." The command does not mean physical withdrawal but spiritual separation. Christians cannot escape living in Babylon, but they must refuse to live *like* Babylon. The danger is not persecution but assimilation—the quiet compromise that dulls devotion. To "come out" is to resist Babylon's values while remaining present as witnesses of the Lamb's kingdom.

Her judgment fits her crimes: "As she glorified herself and lived in luxury, so give her a like measure of torment." The punishment is poetic justice—what she worshiped destroys her.

Lament from earth and rejoicing in heaven (18:9–20)

As Babylon burns, three groups lament her fall—kings, merchants, and sailors. The kings mourn the loss of luxury; the merchants mourn the collapse of trade; the sailors mourn the end of profit. Each laments from a distance, crying, "Alas, alas, for the great city!" Their grief exposes their idolatry. They do not mourn Babylon's sin but their own loss. Babylon's economy traded not only in goods but in "human souls" (18:13). Greed always dehumanizes; idolatry always exploits.

In contrast, heaven rejoices. "Rejoice over her, O heaven, and you saints and apostles and prophets, for God has given judgment for you against her!" The destruction that earth laments is the vindication heaven celebrates. Divine judgment is not vindictive but restorative—it ends oppression and affirms that righteousness matters. Babylon's ruin is good news for those she persecuted. Revelation contrasts the world's mourning with the church's joy, asking believers to align their hearts with heaven's perspective.

The fall of Babylon is the gospel's social consequence. Wherever the gospel thrives, Babylon trembles, for the kingdom of Christ dismantles every false security built on wealth, exploitation, or pride.

The millstone and the silence (18:21–24)

The vision closes with a dramatic symbol. A mighty angel picks up a great millstone and hurls it into the sea, saying, "So will Babylon the great city be thrown down with violence, and will be found no more." The image recalls

Jeremiah 51:63–64, where Babylon's doom is pictured the same way. The city that once dazzled with music, trade, and celebration becomes utterly silent. The list of what disappears—music, craftsmanship, weddings, and light—illustrates total desolation.

Babylon's judgment is not arbitrary. "In her was found the blood of prophets and saints." Her prosperity was built on persecution, her luxury on injustice. God's justice silences her not because he despises culture, but because he refuses to let sin stand unchallenged. The silence after the music is not empty—it is holy. Evil's last note fades, and heaven's song begins.

The fall of Babylon and the faithfulness of the church

Revelation 17–18 is not merely a prophecy of Rome's fall; it is a timeless warning to the church. Babylon still lives wherever wealth becomes worship, politics becomes idolatry, or pleasure replaces purpose. The faithful must live as citizens of a different kingdom, resisting Babylon's seductions with the endurance of those who already know the end of the story.

"Come out of her" does not mean retreat from society but refusal to adopt its idols. Christians engage the world as witnesses, not as worshipers of its systems. They work, build, and bless their communities while remembering that every empire eventually crumbles. The Lamb's victory calls for discernment—an alertness that refuses to confuse comfort with faithfulness.

The contrast between Babylon's fall and the saints' song prepares us for Revelation 19, where heaven rejoices and the Lamb's wedding feast begins. Judgment gives way to celebration; the prostitute's fall makes room for the bride's glory.

The lesson is as urgent now as it was in the first century: the church must choose its city. Will we build our lives on Babylon's promises or on Zion's foundation? The former ends in ruin; the latter ends in rejoicing. The Lamb's people endure because they belong to a kingdom that will never fall.

APPLICATION

1. Babylon still lives wherever idolatry thrives

Revelation's Babylon is not just Rome or some future empire—it is every system that exalts power, wealth, or pleasure above God. Babylon's beauty deceives because it cloaks rebellion in refinement. She sings the song of self-sufficiency: "I sit as queen, and I will never mourn." Christians must learn to discern her voice in modern forms—consumerism that replaces generosity, politics that demands devotion, entertainment that dulls conscience. The call to "come out of her" is a summons to spiritual clarity. We resist Babylon not by isolation but by faithfulness—refusing to adopt her loves or her lies. The gospel calls believers to live as citizens of a better city, whose foundations are righteousness and truth, not greed and pride. Babylon's splendor fades, but the Lamb's kingdom endures forever.

2. God's judgment is justice, not cruelty

The fall of Babylon confronts a common misconception: that divine wrath contradicts divine love. In Revelation, judgment flows from holiness, not hatred. Babylon's luxury was built on exploitation; her glory came from bloodshed. For God to be good, he must end evil. The cries of the saints beneath the altar find their answer here—God's justice defends the innocent and exposes the guilty. Heaven's rejoicing over Babylon's fall is not callous triumph but worshipful relief that truth has prevailed. Judgment reveals what love demands: that oppression cease, idolatry end, and righteousness reign. Christians should proclaim this not with arrogance but with awe. The destruction of Babylon is the vindication of the cross—the final act of a God who will not let evil have the last word.

3. Faithfulness means resisting seduction, not just persecution

Revelation 17–18 warns that the church's greatest danger is not violence from the beast but attraction to Babylon. Persecution tests our courage, but prosperity tests our loyalty. The saints who endure do so because they refuse compromise even when it promises comfort. Faithful discipleship requires discernment: recognizing when cultural norms contradict Christ's kingdom. The call to "come out" is not withdrawal from the world but refusal to be shaped by its idols. The church must embody an alternative economy of grace—valuing generosity over greed, service over status, holiness over indulgence. The fall of Babylon reminds believers that compromise with sin may be profitable now, but it is ruinous forever.

4. The church's hope rests in the Lamb's unshakable kingdom

When Babylon falls, the world mourns the loss of its idols. But the saints rejoice, not out of vengeance, but because the victory of truth has arrived. The fall of the great city is not the end of history—it is the unveiling of God's eternal reign. Revelation reminds believers that their hope is not tied to the rise or fall of nations but to the sovereignty of Christ. His kingdom is not built by commerce or conquest, but by covenant and cross. Therefore, the church must measure success not by influence or wealth but by faithfulness. Babylon's monuments crumble, but the Lamb's throne endures. To live in hope is to sing heaven's song now, trusting that one day the silence of Babylon will give way to the eternal music of the redeemed.

CONCLUSION

The fall of Babylon exposes the emptiness of every human system that exalts itself against God. Her luxury, power, and influence dazzled the world, but her downfall was inevitable. Revelation shows that evil eventually destroys itself, while God's justice restores what Babylon corrupted. For believers, this vision is not a call to fear but to faithfulness—to live distinct from the world's idols and devoted to the Lamb. The command to "come out of her" remains urgent in every generation. When Babylon's music fades, the church's song of victory continues. The kingdoms of the world will crumble, but the Lamb's kingdom endures, and those who follow him will share in his everlasting reign.

REFLECTION

1. What qualities made Babylon so attractive to the nations and so dangerous to believers?

2. How do modern societies reflect the same arrogance and idolatry described in Babylon's fall?

3. What does God's judgment on Babylon reveal about his character and holiness?

4. Why is the command to "come out of her" still relevant for Christians today?

5. How does this vision challenge your personal loyalties and definition of success?

6. What hope do you find in knowing that the Lamb's kingdom will outlast every empire?

DISCUSSION

1. How can believers recognize and resist the seductive power of modern "Babylon"?

2. In what ways does Revelation 17–18 redefine our understanding of God's justice?

3. What dangers arise when the church becomes too comfortable with culture's values?

4. How can Christians live faithfully within society without sharing in its corruption?

5. Why does heaven rejoice at Babylon's downfall, and what does that teach us about worship?

6. What practical steps help a congregation embody loyalty to the Lamb over worldly power?

12

THE MARRIAGE & THE MILLENNIUM

REVELATION 19-20

Objective: To inspire Christians to celebrate Christ's victory and live confidently under his present and eternal reign.

INTRODUCTION

In 1945, as World War II ended, the streets of London erupted in celebration. Crowds filled Trafalgar Square, church bells rang, and strangers embraced—victory had come, and tyranny was over. Yet even in the joy, the world bore deep scars, and much rebuilding lay ahead. Triumph and toil stood side by side.

Revelation 19-20 captures a similar paradox. Heaven rejoices with hallelujahs as the Lamb triumphs over Babylon, yet the story also reveals the ongoing struggle against evil until its final defeat. The wedding feast and the battlefield, the celebration and the judgment, unfold together. The church is called not to fear these visions but to join heaven's praise and live with confidence in Christ's victory.

The marriage supper celebrates the covenant completed, and the millennium affirms the reign already begun. The dragon's doom and the saints' vindication remind believers that the cross secured what eternity will complete. History's final chapters do not describe chaos, but closure—the triumph of truth, the vindication of faith, and the eternal union between the Lamb and his people.

EXAMINATION

Heaven's hallelujahs and the wedding feast (19:1–10)

After the smoke of Babylon rises, John hears the sound of heaven erupting in praise. The opening verses of chapter 19 form one of the most jubilant moments in Revelation: "Hallelujah! Salvation and glory and power belong to our God, for his judgments are true and just." Four hallelujahs resound—praise for judgment, for justice, for victory, and for the Lamb's eternal reign. Heaven rejoices not because of destruction but because righteousness has prevailed. Evil's collapse is not tragedy; it is triumph.

The imagery shifts from the courtroom to the wedding banquet. "The marriage of the Lamb has come, and his Bride has made herself ready." Throughout Scripture, marriage symbolizes covenant fidelity between God and his people (Hos. 2; Eph. 5). The church is the Bride, now purified and prepared, clothed "with fine linen, bright and pure"—the righteous deeds of the saints, made possible by grace. This moment fulfills every promise of redemption. The long engagement of faith now gives way to union and celebration. The angel declares, "Blessed are those who are invited to the marriage supper of the Lamb."

John is so overwhelmed that he falls to worship the angel, but the angel stops him: "Worship God." The correction is vital. Even in glory, Revelation warns against misplaced devotion. The focus remains on the Lamb, not the messenger. The church's destiny is not escape but intimacy—the joy of eternal communion with Christ, her faithful Bridegroom.

The rider on the white horse (19:11–21)

Heaven opens again, and John beholds a warrior riding a white horse. The figure is Christ himself, revealed not as a fragile lamb but as the conquering Word of God. His titles—Faithful and True—declare his reliability and righteousness. His eyes burn with omniscience; his many crowns signify ultimate authority. His robe is dipped in blood, not that of his enemies but his own, symbolizing victory through sacrifice. The sword that proceeds from his mouth represents his word—truth as both weapon and judgment.

The armies of heaven follow him, clothed in white linen, but none carry weapons. Their victory depends solely on their King. The language of battle here, like much of Revelation's imagery, is symbolic. Christ conquers not by violence but by his word, not by bloodshed but by blood given. The "sharp sword" of truth strikes down nations that have opposed him.

The beast and the false prophet—the political and religious systems that deceived the world—are captured and thrown into the lake of fire, symbols of complete and irreversible judgment. The imagery dramatizes a theological truth: every power that exalts itself above God will fall. The Lamb's victory is not postponed to the future; it is the eternal reality of his cross and resurrection. History's final conflict reveals what has always been true—Christ reigns.

The binding of Satan and the reign of the saints (20:1–6)

John next sees an angel descending from heaven, holding a key and a great chain. He seizes the dragon—"that ancient serpent, who is the devil and Satan"—and binds him for a thousand years. This "millennium" has generated endless speculation, but Revelation uses the number symbolically, not chronologically. In apocalyptic language, a thousand signifies fullness or completeness. Satan's binding began with Christ's victory at the cross. Jesus spoke of binding the strong man (Mark 3:27) and declared that the ruler of this world was being cast out (John 12:31).

During this period—the present church age—Satan's power is restrained. He cannot prevent the spread of the gospel or deceive the nations into halting God's mission. Evil still operates, but under limits. The saints, meanwhile, share in the Lamb's reign. John sees "thrones, and seated on them were those to whom authority to judge was committed." These are believers—especially martyrs—who "came to life and reigned with Christ for a thousand years." The "first resurrection" refers to spiritual rebirth and vindication, not physical resurrection. Those who share it are immune to the "second death," the eternal separation from God.

This vision offers assurance, not a timetable. The church's suffering is real, but Christ's reign is already in effect. The saints reign with him through faith, prayer, and perseverance. The millennium is not a pause between comings but the present reality of the gospel age—the Lamb reigning through his people as they bear witness in a hostile world.

The final rebellion and the defeat of Satan (20:7-10)

When the thousand years are complete—that is, when God's redemptive plan reaches its conclusion—Satan is released for a brief time. This "release" represents a final outbreak of evil before the end, a moment when deception and rebellion surge once more. The nations, described as "Gog and Magog," assemble for battle, encompassing "the camp of the saints and the beloved city." The names come from Ezekiel 38-39, where they symbolize the collective enemies of God's people.

Yet the battle never occurs. "Fire came down from heaven and consumed them." Evil's last rebellion is crushed in an instant. Satan is cast into the lake of fire, joining the beast and the false prophet, to be tormented "day and night forever and ever." The vision underscores the finality of evil's defeat. What began in Genesis with the serpent's deception ends here with the serpent's destruction.

This is not a vision of endless violence but of divine closure. Evil's existence, long tolerated for the sake of redemption, ends forever. The dragon's fall confirms that history's outcome was never in doubt. God's sovereignty is total; his justice is complete. The enemy who once accused the saints is silenced for eternity.

The great white throne and final judgment (20:11-15)

John now sees a great white throne and the one seated upon it. "From his presence earth and sky fled away, and no place was found for them." The imagery conveys absolute authority and unapproachable holiness. All the dead, great and small, stand before God. Books are opened, and judgment is rendered "according to what they had done." The sea, death, and Hades give up their dead—no one escapes accountability.

Another book is opened: the book of life. Those whose names are written in it belong to the Lamb and share his life. Judgment is not an arbitrary sentence but a revelation of truth. The books disclose deeds; the book of life discloses relationship. Those who trusted the Lamb are safe, not because their record is flawless but because their names are written by grace.

Death and Hades themselves are thrown into the lake of fire, called "the second death." The greatest enemy is no more. Evil is unmade, and creation stands ready for renewal. The vision's purpose is not to terrify but to vindicate. Justice is not a threat to believers—it is their hope fulfilled.

The Lamb's triumph and the believer's assurance

Revelation 19–20 portrays the final victory of Christ from three angles—celebration, conquest, and consummation. Heaven celebrates with the marriage supper; Christ conquers the beasts; and God consummates redemption through judgment. The structure mirrors the gospel itself: joy, victory, and completion.

The saints celebrate the Lamb's covenant faithfulness; the rider on the white horse embodies his triumph; and the great white throne displays his perfect justice. Every power opposed to God—political, spiritual, or personal—meets its end. The church's role throughout is not to fight but to worship, to persevere, and to trust that the Lamb's word is enough.

The millennium, properly understood, reinforces the church's present calling. Christ reigns now, and his people share in that reign through faithful witness. The enemy is bound, but his final fury reminds us that resistance continues until the end. Still, the church need not fear. The same voice that said, "It is finished," will one day declare, "Behold, I am making all things new."

Revelation 19–20 lifts the believer's eyes from speculation to celebration. The focus is not on deciphering timelines but on trusting the one who holds time in his hands. The saints' endurance and the Lamb's authority assure the church that history's outcome is certain. The wedding feast awaits, the rider still reigns, and the serpent's end is sealed.

APPLICATION

1. Worship is the church's victory cry

The four hallelujahs in Revelation 19 remind believers that worship is heaven's first response to victory. The saints do not celebrate violence but righteousness—the vindication of truth and the faithfulness of God. Worship, then, is not escape from the world's problems but resistance against despair. When Christians praise God amid uncertainty, they declare that the Lamb reigns and Babylon has fallen. Worship aligns the church with heaven's perspective and strengthens endurance on earth. Every song of faith becomes a small rehearsal of the marriage supper of the Lamb. The church's greatest weapon is not power or protest but praise, for worship testifies that Christ's authority is already absolute, even when the world seems unshaken by his rule.

2. The Lamb conquers through his word and sacrifice

The rider on the white horse wields a sword from his mouth—not a weapon of steel but a word of truth. His robe, already dipped in blood, shows that victory comes not by conquest but by the cross. This imagery teaches believers that the way of Christ is not domination but self-giving love. The church's task is not to imitate the beast's methods but to reflect the Lamb's character. Faithfulness may look like weakness, but it is God's chosen means of triumph. Every time believers speak truth, forgive enemies, or serve with humility, they participate in the Lamb's victory. Evil falls not when it is overpowered, but when it is outloved. The word of God, spoken and lived, remains the sharpest sword in history.

3. The millennium calls for confidence, not curiosity

John's vision of the "thousand years" has too often been treated as a puzzle to solve rather than a promise to trust. The millennium symbolizes Christ's present reign—real, active, and complete, though not yet visible in its fullness. Believers live in that reality now, sharing in his authority as they bear witness in the world. Satan is bound, but his influence persists through deception. The church's hope is not in predicting when Christ will reign but in knowing that he reigns already. This perspective frees Christians from fear and speculation. Our confidence rests not in charts or timelines, but in the character of the Lamb. The millennium reminds the church that every act of faithfulness is participation in Christ's current and certain rule.

4. Judgment completes redemption, not contradicts it

The great white throne scene closes the story of evil with perfect balance. The same justice that condemned the beast and the dragon also vindicates the saints. Judgment is not opposed to mercy—it fulfills it. God's justice means that evil does not endure, and grace means that those written in the book of life need not fear. Christians can face the future without anxiety because their names are secured by the blood of the Lamb. Judgment day is not dread for the faithful but deliverance—the moment when God's righteousness is fully revealed and creation's wounds are finally healed. Until that day, the church proclaims both warning and hope: that every knee will bow, every wrong will be righted, and the Lamb's reign will be forever just and good.

CONCLUSION

Revelation 19–20 lifts the church's eyes above fear and speculation to worship and assurance. The marriage supper of the Lamb celebrates the completion of God's covenant love, while the vision of the rider on the white horse proclaims that Christ already reigns in power and truth. The millennium reminds believers that his kingdom is present now, even as they await its full unveiling. Satan's final defeat and the great white throne judgment reveal that justice and mercy will both be complete. For those who follow the Lamb, the future is not uncertain—it is sealed. The final word belongs to Christ, and his promise stands: those who share his cross will also share his crown.

REFLECTION

1. How does the marriage supper of the Lamb deepen your understanding of salvation and fellowship with Christ?

2. What does the rider's bloodstained robe teach about the nature of true victory?

3. Why is it important to see the "thousand years" as symbolic of Christ's present reign?

4. How does knowing Satan's defeat strengthen your courage to endure spiritual opposition?

5. What emotions arise as you picture the great white throne and the book of life?

6. How does Revelation 19–20 give you confidence in God's justice and mercy?

DISCUSSION

1. What can the church today learn from heaven's hallelujahs after Babylon's fall?

2. How should Christ's method of conquering—through truth and sacrifice—shape Christian witness?

3. In what ways does Revelation challenge popular views of power, success, and authority?

4. How can Christians live as participants in Christ's present reign rather than spectators of history?

5. Why should final judgment inspire both reverence and hope for the people of God?

6. What practices help your congregation worship and witness with confidence in the Lamb's victory?

13

THE NEW HEAVEN & NEW EARTH

REVELATION 21-22

Objective: To encourage Christians to live with hope, anticipating God's renewal of creation and eternal fellowship with him.

INTRODUCTION

In 1948, a young British soldier named Leonard Cheshire returned from World War II haunted by what he'd seen. He devoted the rest of his life to caring for the sick and dying. When asked why, he said, "I wanted to build a place where broken people could begin again." His longing mirrored humanity's deepest hope—the desire for renewal, not merely repair.

That longing finds its ultimate answer in Revelation 21–22. John's final vision unveils not escape from the world but its restoration. The old creation, scarred by sin and death, gives way to a new heaven and a new earth. The holy city descends, not as a monument of human achievement but as a gift of divine grace. God himself dwells with his people, and the curse is gone forever.

The story that began with exile from Eden ends with homecoming to God. Every tear is wiped away, every fracture mended, and every shadow replaced by light. Revelation closes not with speculation about the future but with certainty about the present hope: the Lamb reigns, creation will be renewed, and the invitation still stands—"Come."

EXAMINATION

A new heaven and a new earth (21:1-8)

John's final vision begins not with destruction but with renewal. "Then I saw a new heaven and a new earth, for the first heaven and the first earth had passed away." As Isaiah foretold, God says, "Behold, I create new heavens and a new earth" (Isa. 65:17). The sea, long a symbol of chaos, danger, and rebellion, is "no more." The restless forces that once threatened God's people are gone forever.

John sees "the holy city, new Jerusalem, coming down out of heaven from God, prepared as a bride adorned for her husband." Heaven descends; creation is united with its Creator. God's dwelling place is now among his people. The separation between heaven and earth is healed. The voice from the throne proclaims the heart of the gospel's promise: "Behold, the dwelling place of God is with man. He will dwell with them, and they will be his people." What Israel experienced in the tabernacle and temple now fills all creation.

Every trace of sorrow disappears. "He will wipe away every tear from their eyes, and death shall be no more." The former things—sin, grief, decay—have passed away. The one seated on the throne declares, "Behold, I am making all things new." Notice the tense: not *I will make*, but *I am making*. The work of new creation has already begun in Christ's resurrection and will be completed at his return.

The Alpha and Omega, the beginning and the end, promises, "To the thirsty I will give from the spring of the water of life without payment." Grace remains the foundation of eternal life—it is still given freely. Those who overcome will inherit this new creation, but "the cowardly, the faithless, the detestable" face the second death. The distinction between the faithful and the unfaithful endures, but the invitation remains open. The Lamb's victory makes all things new, yet it calls every heart to choose which world it will belong to.

The bride, the new Jerusalem (21:9-27)

One of the angels who had poured out the bowls of judgment now shows John "the Bride, the wife of the Lamb." The same angel who displayed Babylon's corruption now reveals the Bride's beauty—the perfect counterpart.

Babylon seduced the nations with her immorality; the new Jerusalem draws them with her holiness. Evil's city has fallen; God's city descends.

The holy city shines "with the glory of God, its radiance like a most rare jewel." The vision combines images of a city, a bride, and a temple—all metaphors for the people of God in perfect communion with him. The walls, gates, and foundations gleam with precious stones, echoing the high priest's breastplate (Exod. 28:17–21). The names of Israel's tribes and the apostles are inscribed, uniting old covenant and new. God's redeemed people, from every age, now dwell together in holiness.

The city's measurements are striking: twelve thousand stadia in length, width, and height—a perfect cube, recalling the Holy of Holies. What was once hidden behind a veil now fills all creation. There is no temple in the city, "for its temple is the Lord God the Almighty and the Lamb." Worship no longer requires mediation or sacred space; the entire cosmos is sanctified by God's presence. The glory of God illuminates the city, and "its lamp is the Lamb."

The nations walk by its light, and kings bring their glory into it. This does not depict separate realms but the inclusion of all peoples redeemed by grace. The treasures of culture and creation—purged of corruption—are brought before God in worship. The gates remain perpetually open; nothing unclean will ever enter. The story that began in Eden's exile ends in perfect welcome. The light of God replaces the shadow of death, and humanity's true home is restored.

The river and the tree of life (22:1–5)

John's vision moves from the city to its center, where "the river of the water of life, bright as crystal, flows from the throne of God and of the Lamb." This river fulfills Ezekiel 47, where life-giving waters flow from the temple to renew creation. Here, the source is no longer a building but God himself. From his throne flows unending vitality and joy.

On each side of the river grows the tree of life, bearing twelve kinds of fruit, yielding fruit every month. In Eden, access to the tree was barred after the fall; now, through the Lamb, it is freely available. The tree's leaves are "for the healing of the nations." The imagery does not suggest ongoing disease but continual flourishing. Redemption restores what sin fractured—between God and humanity, between nations, and between creation and creator.

John declares, "No longer will there be anything accursed." The curse that began in Genesis 3 is undone. "The throne of God and of the Lamb will be in it, and his servants will worship him." To "see his face" fulfills the deepest longing of Scripture—what Moses could not behold (Exod. 33:20) is now granted to every believer. God's name is written on their foreheads, signifying ownership, identity, and intimacy. Night will be no more, for the Lord God will be their light, and they will reign with him forever.

The redeemed do not drift through eternity as spectators; they reign as partners in God's restored creation. The story of Scripture comes full circle: humanity, once driven from Eden, now rules again under God's loving authority. The Lamb's work does not end with salvation from sin—it extends to the renewal of vocation, community, and creation itself.

The final invitation and benediction (22:6–21)

The vision closes with affirmation and appeal. "These words are trustworthy and true," says the angel, confirming that Revelation is not imagination but revelation. The message comes from "the Lord, the God of the spirits of the prophets," tying John's vision to the long line of biblical prophecy. Jesus himself speaks: "Behold, I am coming soon." The promise of his return frames the church's hope and defines its mission.

Three themes dominate the conclusion: *truth, urgency,* and *invitation.* Truth—because God's word is reliable. Urgency—because Christ's return is imminent. Invitation—because grace remains open to all. The Spirit and the Bride together cry, "Come!" Their joint voice embodies the church's mission: to invite the thirsty to receive the water of life freely. Even at the book's end, the gospel's door stands wide open.

John falls again in worship before the angel and again is corrected: "Worship God." Revelation insists that no messenger, miracle, or mystery should distract from the Maker. The vision concludes with warning: do not add to or subtract from the prophecy, for it speaks complete truth. The final word of Jesus resounds, "Surely I am coming soon." And John replies on behalf of the church, "Amen. Come, Lord Jesus!"

The book closes not with fear, but with friendship: "The grace of the Lord Jesus be with all. Amen." The same grace that began the story sustains it to the end. From the first page of Genesis to the final line of Revelation,

God's purpose has been communion—creation dwelling with Creator in joy, holiness, and peace.

The hope of new creation

Revelation 21–22 gives voice to humanity's deepest longing and God's oldest promise. What began with separation ends with union; what began with curse ends with blessing. The Bible's story, from Eden to new Jerusalem, is not a tale of escape from earth but of earth's renewal. The Lamb does not abandon creation; he redeems it.

Revelation shows that the gospel's goal is not speculation about heaven's geography but transformation of life on earth. The church lives as a preview of this new creation—its worship a foretaste, its love a reflection, its witness an invitation. Christians endure suffering because they know the ending: the Lamb wins, and his people dwell with him forever.

Revelation's closing chapters are not fantasy but fulfillment. They remind the church that history is headed toward healing, not chaos. The same God who once walked with Adam now walks again with his children. The river flows, the tree flourishes, and the Lamb's name shines on every face. The story ends not with a period, but with a promise: "Surely I am coming soon." Until that day, the Spirit and the Bride still say, "Come."

APPLICATION

1. God's goal is renewal, not escape

John's vision reminds believers that redemption is not about leaving the world behind but about God making all things new. The gospel is cosmic in scope—what Christ began in his resurrection, he will finish in new creation. The Christian hope is not floating among the clouds but dwelling with God in a restored heaven and earth. This perspective transforms how we live now. Our work, our worship, and our witness all participate in that renewal. Every act of faithfulness, compassion, and justice anticipates the day when God's presence fills everything. The church's mission is to live as a preview of that future—to show the world what new creation looks like through lives shaped by holiness, mercy, and joy. We don't wait for heaven to start living the life of heaven now.

2. The Lamb's presence fulfills every longing

The promise "God will dwell with them" lies at the heart of Revelation's final vision. Humanity's deepest ache—to see God's face and be fully known—is finally satisfied. Heaven is not defined by gold or glory but by intimacy with the Lamb. For weary Christians, this promise redefines perseverance. Every tear, every trial, every act of faith in the dark will one day give way to unbroken fellowship with Christ. The bride's beauty comes not from her own adornment but from her nearness to her Bridegroom. This truth invites believers to live with longing rather than fear. We are not waiting for the end of the world but for the fullness of communion. Worship is how the church rehearses that joy even while we wait.

3. The call to holiness continues until he comes

Twice in Revelation 22, Jesus says, "Behold, I am coming soon." That promise calls believers to readiness. The new Jerusalem is pure because God's presence allows nothing unclean. The church must therefore live as the bride preparing for her wedding, keeping garments unspotted by Babylon's seductions. Holiness is not withdrawal from the world but loyalty to the Lamb amid it. The same grace that welcomes us also transforms us. Our daily faithfulness—our speech, our service, our repentance—becomes part of that preparation. Revelation's closing command, "Come out of her, my people," now finds its fulfillment in "Come, Lord Jesus." Until he returns, we pursue purity not from fear of judgment but from the joy of expectation. The bride readies herself by loving what her Bridegroom loves.

4. The story ends with invitation and grace

Revelation's final word is not wrath but welcome. "The Spirit and the Bride say, 'Come.'" Even at the end of Scripture, God's heart remains open to the thirsty. This invitation defines the church's mission—extending grace to a world that still wanders. We live between two comings: the invitation for sinners to draw near and the promise that Christ will return. Both are expressions of mercy. Until that day, our calling is to echo the Spirit's voice—inviting others to drink freely from the water of life. The book closes as the Bible began: with grace offered to all who will receive it. The final verse, "The grace of the Lord Jesus be with all," assures believers that the same grace which began creation will sustain and complete its renewal.

CONCLUSION

Revelation closes with promise and peace. The Lamb who conquered evil now reigns among his people, and creation itself is renewed. The separation between heaven and earth is gone; God's dwelling is with humanity forever. The curse is broken, the river flows freely, and the tree of life bears fruit for all nations. The story that began in a garden ends in a city—holy, radiant, and filled with God's glory. Every longing of faith finds its fulfillment here. Until that day, the church lives in hope, echoing the Spirit's invitation: "Come." The last word of Scripture is not judgment but grace—the enduring promise that the Lord Jesus is coming soon.

REFLECTION

1. What does it mean that God is making "all things new" rather than "all new things"?

2. How does the image of the new Jerusalem as a bride deepen your understanding of the church?

3. Why is God's presence—"He will dwell with them"—the central joy of eternity?

4. What do the river and tree of life reveal about God's purpose for creation?

5. How does this vision of restoration give hope to those living in a broken world?

6. What response does the repeated promise "I am coming soon" stir in your heart?

DISCUSSION

1. How can the church embody the hope of new creation in its worship and daily life?

2. What aspects of Babylon's world still tempt believers away from loyalty to the Lamb?

3. Why is the book of Revelation's ending more about invitation than fear?

4. How might understanding the new heaven and earth reshape your view of heaven itself?

5. What does it look like to live as citizens of the new Jerusalem while still on earth?

6. How can we echo the Spirit and the Bride's invitation to "Come" in our communities today?

www.ingramcontent.com/pod-product-compliance
Lightning Source LLC
Chambersburg PA
CBHW070153080526
44586CB00015B/1965